THE MEANING OF EUROPE

BY Denis de Rougemont

TRANSLATED FROM THE FRENCH BY ALAN BRALEY, F.I.L.

The Meaning

of Europe

STEIN AND DAY/*Publishers*/New York

First published in England by Sidgwick and Jackson, 1965
First published in the United States of America 1965
Copyright © Denis de Rougemont 1963
Library of Congress Catalog Card No. 65-22272
All rights reserved
Printed in the United States of America
Stein and Day/Publishers/7 East 48 Street, New York, N.Y. 10017

CONTENTS

FOREWORD

THE LECTURES reproduced in this small volume were
delivered in the Aula at Geneva University in the
studium generale series intended for students of all facul-
ties and open to the public. Their subject was suggested to me by Professor Eric Martin, rector of the
University, to whom I here express my thanks. In
inviting me to occupy, on four Thursdays in May,
this chair which may be compared in more than one
respect with the "danger-seat" spoken of in British
novels, he was offering me a fascinatingly difficult
exercise. To deal in a few brief lectures with the adventure of Europe covering more than two millennia
is in itself an adventure fraught with some risk. Moreover, one had to give a reply to the question which
was implicit in the title, and to hazard a forecast of
developments in Europe in the near future, to a
young audience which in some ways I believed tended
to disregard any interpretation save that of an in-
soluble crisis, expressed in the jargon which was
fashionable a short time ago. In this latter respect I
was mistaken. The patience and goodwill of my stu-
dent audience finally convinced me of this. To them,
then, I dedicate these four short essays on the hopes
of Europe.

D. DE R.

I

THE WORLDWIDE ADVENTURE
OF THE EUROPEANS

I

THE WORLDWIDE ADVENTURE
OF THE EUROPEANS

The Phenomenon of Europe
defined by its effects

I wish to speak to you about Europe, not as a cause to defend or a larger homeland to glorify, but as *an adventure of decisive significance for the whole of mankind.* By Europe, I mean that part of the world which *made* "the World", since it was in Europe that the idea of "the human race" was born; in fact Europe was the *sine qua non* of a truly universal history, something in which we are well and truly involved in this second half of the 20th century; so that henceforth, for practical purposes, the future prospects for Europe are inextricably bound up with those of the civilisation brought into being by her actions, propagated by her without thought of consequences or any unified plan, and which she no longer owns, though some of its vital secrets remain in her keeping. I have only four lectures in which to establish this central thesis, *this definition of Europe in functional terms as the "creator of the world."* This means defining the phenomenon of Europe by its *effects*, whereas up to the present the attempt has always been made to explain Europe by *causes* which, according to the author or the theory consulted, might be geographical, climatic, economic or demographic.

11

What I call the phenomenon of Europe has, when seen in the scale of world history, a number of completely original and distinctive features. Take, for example, the following:

1. Europe discovered the whole of the earth, and nobody ever came and discovered Europe.
2. Europe has held sway on all the continents in succession, and up till now has never been ruled by any foreign power.
3. Europe has produced a civilisation which is being imitated by the whole world, whilst the converse has never happened.

These facts, so simple and obvious that most historians, it seems to me, have so far neglected them, point to something unique. This phenomenon of Europe is without precedent or parallel in history; and we shall never be able to grasp it in its dynamism, its significance and its general direction by starting from the physical and natural features of our small continent. Such an attempt is a survival from nineteenth century modes of thought which, without knowing it, generally owe more to popularisations of marxism than to scientific method. Not that I deny the importance of the natural environment; I simply find it inadequate to account for the specific features of this phenomenon.

Destiny cannot stem from natural endowments

It is true that the indented coastline favourable to navigation, the separation of land areas by mountains and rivers, which favoured the formation of distinct and deeply-rooted communities, and the temperate climate (in the centre, at any rate) allowing vital energies to be conserved, were all natural advantages. But they are far from being a sufficient explanation of our subsequent worldwide rôle. No destiny is to be read in the soil of Europe. Moreover, every geographer draws from it what he pleases. Thus in the fifth century B.C. Hippocrates explained the superiority of Europeans to Asiatics by the fact that the Asiatics lived in a too unvaried climate, whereas, he says, in Europe "the rapid transitions from one extreme to the other force men to think and are inimical to easy-going attitudes."[1] But another Greek, Strabo, writing at the time of Tiberius, takes the contrary view and attributes this very superiority of Europeans to the temperate climate which "seems to have done everything possible to hasten the progress of civilisation".[2] More realistically, the *Geographie universelle* of Mantelle and Brun, published in Paris in 1816, recognizes that the history of Europe was not determined by its geography. I would like to quote their description of Europe, which I think Valéry had in mind in the famous passage in which he describes Europe as "a kind of promontory of the ancient continent, a western appendix of Asia" but nonetheless "the valuable part of the terrestrial universe, the pearl of the globe, the brain of a vast body". This is the passage:

"When it left the hands of nature, our part of the world had not received any title to that glorious pre-eminence which now distinguishes it. A little continent with few territorial riches . . . only our borrowings have made us rich. Yet, such is the power of the human mind, this region whose sole natural covering was that of immense forests has become inhabited by powerful nations, covered with magnificent cities and

13

enriched with the spoils of the two worlds. This narrow peninsula, which appears on the map as no more than an appendix of Asia, has become the metropolis of the human race".[3]

Here the influence of geography and climate is played down, almost denied. Must we then look to demography for the secret of Europe's expansion? A glance at the map of population densities shows us that for a long time past humanity has been concentrated in three regions which are pre-eminent in this respect: China, India and Europe, each of which in the twentieth century has some 5 to 600 million inhabitants, or a combined total of 60 per cent of the world's population, on 15 per cent of its land surface.[4] But the Europe of the Renaissance, of the Great Discoveries and of worldwide expansion, was very much less populous than China or India, and was not subject to any demographic pressure, even in the most prosperous and enterprising countries on the continent. Thus, Charles Morazé says that the population of France hardly changed between 1328 and 1700, being ten million at the most. The explosive population increase on our continent dates only from the nineteenth century. Then how is it that India, another Asian peninsula more or less comparable in extent to Western Europe but far richer in men and raw materials, offers the historian little beyond the spectacle of centuries-old decline, at the very time when Europe was encircling the world and gaining the mastery over most of its peoples, including India? In 1850 the Chinese constituted one-third of the world's population; they still form nearly a quarter of it, though by A.D. 2000, according to demographers, they will be only one-fifth —a forecast which runs counter to the fears prevalent in the West. Why, then, have the Chinese played hardly any part in world history, except by their ability to be conquered and to absorb their conquerors, whether Huns or Mongols?

Since the destiny of Europe cannot be explained through physical and natural causes, should we seek the explanation in spiritual causes? Was Europe, for example, created by Christianity, as a very numerous contemporary school of excellent Catholic historians maintains? This is a debatable thesis. We have just seen that Hippocrates and Strabo discussed Europe, and even contrasted it with Asia. Herodotus, Plato and Aristotle did the same—at a time when Christianity was still unknown to Europe. The missionary expansion of Christians during the first thousand years of our era took place in obedience to the Command of Christ: "Go ye into all the world and make disciples of all nations". This command has sent those who accept it to the most distant corners of the earth, from the 4th century onwards. They have gone to North Africa and South India, to the coast of Malabar and even to the Far East (there were more than sixty Nestorian bishops in China in the ninth century under the T'ang dynasty) and to the West, to Iceland, to Labrador, to North America, and perhaps even as far as the Yucatan of the Mayas and to the Peru of the Incas. But this was a Christian expansion, not a specifically European one. The colonialist expansion, on the other hand, of the eighteenth to twentieth centuries, was quite obviously more European than Christian. To equate Europe with Christianity, as Novalis tried to do in his famous essay entitled *Die Christenheit oder Europa* (Christianity or Europe) is to do an injustice to the universal claims of

Christianity without defining Europe, since it means defining Europe by an eternal truth of which she is not a fitting embodiment and in which she has no copyright.

The fact remains that Christianity has made a very strong contribution to the European synthesis. Our idea of science derives from it, as Jaspers has shown when commenting on Nietzsche, that very lucid anti-Christian; and our political principles derive from it. Moreover, there is no doubt that our scientific ideas and our principles of equality, liberty and justice have played a decisive part in Europe's adventure into the world. Christianity, then, is certainly one element which we shall keep sight of in this rapid enquiry into the origins of the European phenomenon; but not without asking ourselves a difficult question, which I shall leave unanswered: why was Europe the only, or the first, part of the world to adopt this religion—which came from the Near East and not from Europe itself? The mystery is as stubborn as ever. And the other explanations of the European phenomenon by reference to its physical and material attributes provide us with no clear answer. Each of these facts has made its own contribution, but none of them appears adequate to explain the global phenomenon with which history confronts us: the worldwide function of Europe.

We shall now describe this phenomenon as the record shows it. It is not the logical process of a series of natural causes producing effects and then losing their impetus. Neither is it the incarnation of some platonic Idea, nor the outward manifestation of some hegelian Spirit moving on with measured dialectic tread—thesis, anti-thesis, synthesis; one, two, one, two. On the contrary it is an Adventure which, though still unfinished, manifests throughout a certain consistent attitude towards life.

In the nineteenth century a phenomenon was always explained by its causes, often at the cost of misunderstanding the phenomenon itself. We of the twentieth century know that a phenomenon, whether individual or collective, can be properly understood only in its creative movement, its archetype, its myth.

For me, this creative *movement* of Europe is found right at the outset in the original legend of the carrying away of Europa by Zeus.

The Europe of the legend begins with a leap towards the West, the sea and adventure. The myth of the abduction of a Tyrian princess by the high God of the Greeks transformed into a bull, is a paraphrase of history; our Europe did indeed come from the Near East. After the almost total disappearance of the "first inhabitants of wood and rock" as Vigny puts it, whose only memorial are the rock paintings of Lascaux and Altamira, Europe was slowly repopulated by colonists from somewhere in Asia Minor along the Vardar and the Danube, as far as the Rhineland and France. Others came from the Nile Delta and settled along the coasts, (ascending the Rhone as far as Switzerland), in Northern France and possibly Britain.[8] Civilization was born in Europe by the effect of a succession of intellectual, technical and religious contributions which had their origin in Egypt, Mesopotamia and Phoenicia and were transferred thence first to Crete (where Princess Europa gave birth to a dynasty, the Minoans) then via the Aegean Sea to Greece, and from there to the countries of the West, known in Semitic languages as *Ereb*, which very probably is the derivation of the name Europe.[9]

Later, the religion which was to dominate the continent came to it from the nearest of the countries in the Phoenician coastland whence its eponymous heroine had been carried off, and who had given her name to the contininent.

This is known, but less well known is what followed the creative rapine, the sequel to the myth of the Abduction of Europa—though for my part I attach the greatest symbolical importance to this sequel. Europa was the daughter of Agenor, king of Tyre. He straightway ordered his five sons to set out in quest of their abducted sister, and each one sailed in a different direction. One of them founded Carthage, whilst others discovered the coasts of the continent from Spain to the Caucasus. Finally Cadmus, the most famous of them, went off first to Rhodes and then to Thrace and, in despair of finding his lost sister and bringing her back to her native shores of Asia, went to the Delphic oracle and enquired "Where is Europa?" "You will not find her," replied Pythia. "Your task is to follow a cow, driving her on before you without respite until she falls exhausted. On that spot, build a city." Cadmus founded Thebes.[10]

This fable, like all divine things, is ambiguous, leaving us a wide choice of interpretation and decision. But here is one interpretation. It was by pursuing the mythical image of Europe that the Phoenician seamen discovered her geographical reality. But it was also by ceasing to look for Europe exactly as she lay in his memory that Cadmus set about building her. And ever since that age of fable, how hard it has been to establish "where Europe was to be found", that is if we are talking in terms of abstract principles, of platonic ideas, or of defining her as a complete and given fact of history; for it is the search for Europe which has created her. To seek Europe is to make her! Her existence is in the search for her. Perhaps she is simply an infinite quest, and this I call: *Adventure*.

But Europe is something else as well, if the second legend regarding her origin (that of Japheth) is to be believed. According to commentaries on the Book of Genesis by the Church Fathers, Noah divided the world between his sons, Shem, Ham and Japheth.[11] To Ham he gave Africa, but also slavery, to punish him for having come upon his father in a state of drunken nakedness without thinking, as did his brothers, of covering him with a coat; to Shem he gave Asia and spirituality, and to Japheth Europe and arms, with the promise of boundless expansion: *dilatatio, latitudo*, according to the Vulgate and the Fathers. *Dilatatio*, expansion, is the keyword.

Now let us review the stages by which this worldwide expansion occurred. Seen in the perspective of history, they recall the movements of systole and diastole of the human heart, though of very unequal duration.

The first movement was the *concentration* of the religious and cultural values of the Near East in the Western peninsula. As we have seen, these populations, religions, technical processes and rudiments of science all came from the East towards Europe, and all was gradually concentrated into this kind of cul-de-sac beyond which, it was thought, the world ended. A primary, original culture was formed in Greece, then diffused and transformed by the Roman Empire. For the individualism which held sway in the cities of Greece the Empire substituted the cult of the State and of big, centralized institutions, and it extended their authority over the whole of Western Europe. Within the bounds of this empire were found Celts, Germans and Slavs, an ever-increasing number of "barbarians", and traditions very contrary to those of Rome, which nevertheless were progressively integrated. Lastly it was this empire that provided the framework for the very rapid expansion of a religion which itself came from the Near East via the Mediterranean—Christianity.

And so when the Empire was finished, at the beginning of the Middle Ages proper under Charlemagne, the European peninsula had become the meeting place of seven or eight different traditions—oriental and nordic, contintental and maritime, individualistic and community minded, rationalist and magical. And the task of synthesizing all these forces in latent conflict or open war, this improbable task was undertaken by the Church.

Europe and her culture are the result of this fusion, never complete, always unstable, the great originality of which (compared with the cultures of Asia) consists precisely in its being a dynamic mixture of elements of different origins and conflicting tendencies.

Throughout the Middle Ages and the interactive strife between Church and Empire, emperor, kings and feudal barons, cities and princes, orthodoxy and heresies, this ferment went on as if in a retort, a kind of alchemist's crucible, where the most unexpected reactions took place. And, indeed, the door of the oven was tightly closed; for Islam had appeared in the East, barring the way to the Orient. Europeans found themselves cut off from all regular communication with the civilizations of India and China, the fabulous riches of which were described for them by rare travellers such as Marco Polo, Rubrukis or Jean de Plan-Carpin. Several times, in the Crusades, they tried to break out, but in vain. How were they to force the bolt of Islam, and bring the Good News to the pagan tribes of Asia and Africa? How to escape from these endless wars, these theological and scholastic quarrels which ended, all too often, on the scaffold? How to fulfil the imperial ambitions inherited from Rome, the delirious dreams of learned cosmographers, or the missionary vocation of the faithful? The overland routes were barred. The Ocean paths remained. That is where the worldwide adventure of Europe begins, the morning that Columbus embarked in his little caravels.

The period of the Great Discoveries was a sort of explosion of the European mixture, pent up for nearly a thousand years within the bounds of the western "peninsula", and compressed still further by the Turks in the East and the Arabs in the South-West.

Christopher Columbus did not set out to look for America, for he did not believe it existed and therefore could not have been looking for it. He went to find the fabulous Indies whose cities were said to be paved with gold, and to bring back thence the treasures on which his king was relying to pay for the final Crusade and set Jerusalem free. The archetypal adventure of this Ulysses with the heart of a Christian, probably of Jewish origin, who founded an empire—for others—was played out against a confused background of religious faith, geographical chance and mischance, imperial ambitions, mythical science and nostalgia for the Holy Grail. Everything about him seems to me to illustrate the basic traits of our Europe, at once legendary, historical, physical, pagan and Christian—the mythical man, the sailor, the treasure-hunter, the missionary and crusader. His very name was Colon—colonist—and his first name Christopher, Christ-bearer—in truth, a carrier of the World's history! But for this frenetic adventurer to appear bearing the noble titles of "Viceroy of the Isles which have been discovered in the Indies" and "Grand Admiral of the High Seas", it was necessary that Jason, in an earlier age, should have been in Colchis pursuing a golden Chimaera, that the Western continent should have had better sea connections than any other, that its land should have been poor in metals, that Islam should have captured Jerusalem and gone on to occupy Byzantium, thus closing the route to Asia, and that the Catholic Kings should have been in need of gold, not for themselves but to pay for one last, utopian crusade. Thus we find behind Columbus's incredible daring the complex play, the perpetual and often fruitful conflict, of all the forces which have created the West: Greece, Rome, Jerusalem, Celtic magic, Jewish restlessness, German science and the strain of mysticism in the Iberian race.[12] The mixture of all these elements resulted in the *accidental* discovery of America, and with it the beginning of centuries of expansion—economic, political, and religious—of a small Asian promontory hemmed in by raging seas and Turks, occupying less than five per cent of the earth's land surface and going on to conquer the rest of the world piecemeal.

Starting with Columbus, Europe's worldwide adventure developed at a pace rather like that of a satellite-carrying rocket. The take-off was slow, then acceleration was progressive; successive stages were fired and it went into orbit: then, after circling the globe a number of times, it fell quickly back to earth. But the return of the satellite does not denote failure! A mass of information has been gathered in the process, henceforth to form part not only of human knowledge but of the human conscience, both of which have been for ever enlarged and altered.

We are familiar with these stages fired in succession, these steps in the conquest of terrestrial space by the Europeans. First there was the initial girdling of the globe, accomplished by Magellan, then the conquest of South America, the peopling of North America, the exploration of the coast of Africa, the subjugation of the Near East and then of India in the eighteenth century, the colonisation of Indonesia by the Portuguese and the Dutch, and of the vast spaces of Siberia by the Russians, the opening of the Far East to European civilization in the middle of the nineteenth century, and finally the colonization of Sub-Saharan Africa from 1880 to 1900.

By the beginning of the twentieth century, Europe can be said to have put her civilization into orbit. But, one by one, the stages of the carrier rocket fell back to earth —military conquest, the seizure of political or economic power, and lastly colonization. Century after century the continents which were discovered and ruled by Europe have freed themselves from her tutelage. The first to do so was North America, towards the end of the eighteenth century. Then came Latin America in the first half of the nineteenth century. India, Indonesia, South-East Asia and the Near East followed after the second World War, and lastly, by about 1960, most of Africa.

Europe had begun by forming links between continents which before her time had lived in the most complete ignorance of one another. Through her, the human race became conscious of its unity. The universalist idea, the very idea of a human race—*genus humanum*—are the creations first of Greco-roman Europe, then of Christian Europe and finally of technological Europe. In this sense it may truly be said that "Europe made the world".

But having made the world, she has lost it. The world has rebelled against her in the name of those very values of liberty, justice and equality for all nations, and of respect for the individual whosoever he be, which she herself formulated and propagated without thought of the consequences. So we see her again reduced to herself, confined within the boundaries of her Asian promontory and no larger, let us note carefully, than she was in the Middle Ages. She is still the heart of a West born of her deeds, but in which two great empires are challenging her supremacy, one hostilely, the other as an ally, whilst Africa, Asia and the Arab world endeavour to deploy their renascent strength against the divided West.

Is this the end of the West's Adventure? If so, what it amounts to is that the West made the world, but made it hostile to its makers.

Before even attempting a reply to this question with all its burning topicality, we shall try to summarize the constant characteristics of the European phenomenon in the course which we have traced, and of the spirit which has sustained through the centuries the astonishing dynamism of the West.

To my mind, the passion inspiring this unprecedented adventure is best symbolized by one of the heroes of the oldest Greek poem; I refer to Homer's Ulysses, the central character in the *Odyssey*.

His departure on a species of crusade against Troy, a town in the Near East, in order to save the honour of the West and to recapture Helen, symbol of virtue and beauty, prefigures the missionary ideal which, between fifteen hundred and two thousand years later, was to move the early Church to send out evangelists as far as China to the East and to Iceland and the Atlantic coasts of America to the West.[13] The military victory of the Greeks over the Trojans prefigures the military expeditions of Europeans to the four other continents. That is the *Iliad*, a "poem about power" as Simone Weil aptly called it. But the most typically western thing about the homeric poems is what followed, Ulysses' personal adventure described in the *Odyssey*, that interminable voyage towards original, eternal wisdom, towards his native country of Ithaca; this enthralling tale of a wanderer, these endless peregrinations which were also a prolonged "error" in the Latin and English meaning of the word. For everything that happens throughout this long epic suggests that Ulysses, a brave and resourceful man, secretly prefers the voyage to its destination, the trials of the journey to a blessed arrival, and the never-ending risks to happiness and peace with Penelope. To conquer the elements, to measure his strength against visible and invisible adversaries, to penetrate ever further into the unknown, skilfully guiding his ship between opposite excesses—the Scillas and Charibdis—this is Ulysses' master-passion, and this too was to be the guiding passion of the great creators of western culture. Western man is the man who always goes farther, beyond the limits set by nature, beyond traditions fixed by his ancestors, even beyond himself—*on to adventure!* He transcends his destiny, and even his interests, for the sake of a universal vocation.

Abraham, "the father of them that believe", set out not knowing whither he went, because his God, the truth in his very core, told him to go out into the unknown. He found the country that God had provided for him, and that was the end of his adventure; but it was the beginning of another story, which is far from ended yet. Christopher Columbus, the father of the Discoverers, thought he knew where he was going and what he was looking for. He reckoned he would get there in thirty days. But all his calculations were wrong; he found the Antilles instead of Xipango, and at the end it was his faith alone that kept him going, for the two great problems that he was trying to solve—to reach India by going round the flank of Islam, and to finance the last Crusade—were not solved by his expedition. Like Ulysses he found other lands and other isles, which were to raise fresh and literally incalculable problems. After that, men always had to go further, unable to foresee the consequences—by which I mean without being able to measure the unknown and delayed effects of material discoveries which were to change man's awareness in quite unpredictable ways. For me this acceptance of risk despite the inevitable lack of foreknowledge is the hallmark of the adventure of the West in every sphere of life.

In short, Western savants from Kepler to Einstein, from Leonardo with his flying man to the biologists of to-day with their synthetic man, have been doing exactly the same as Columbus and Ulysses before them; they start out in search of more or less distant goals which they have envisaged to the best of their ability; they were mistaken as to the goals they sought, or the name and nature of their objective: and what they find raises fresh and unexpected problems, upsets long-standing equilibriums, and calls for the rethinking of yesterday's certainties and for more distant searches entailing ever-increasing risks. To push ahead with research, incurring a new risk for every problem solved, this, I believe, is the true formula for Progress as it is defined in the West. And it is, quite obviously, ambiguous. This can be easily shown from the ambiguity of our *technical achievements*. We go faster and faster, but whither? We save time, but what do we do with it? We increase our power, but what of our ability to master it and make it serve the ends of happiness, justice and wisdom?

The essence of the genius of the West, which most clearly illustrates the contrast between the adventurous Western half of the world and the metaphysical genius of the East, is its preference for the ardent pursuit of partial truths, *come what may*—and for creative risk-taking over prudent meditation on immutable wisdom.

Now we shall try to make out what comes next in the European adventure, and see whether another movement of diastole may follow the systole movement which possibly ended recently, with the independence of Algeria. To do this we shall have to consider, in the three succeeding chapters, three kinds of realities:

the *geo-political* situation of Europe in the contemporary world, which she has herself transformed:

the *living strength* which Europe still possesses if she will unite, and the *secrets* which she alone still holds of a civilization which will soon be universal; and lastly:

the *function* which she has yet to fulfil notwithstanding the prophets of her decadence, in a world which hates her above all for having shown it how poor it is, but which sometimes I think I hear whispering in her ear the words that have saved sick people from death: "Put up a fight; you mustn't die; I need you."

NOTES ON CHAPTER I

1. Hippocrates is the first author known to us who described Europe as an entity, contrasting it with Asia in the Treatise entitled *Airs, Waters, Places*, chapter V, which dates from the end of the fifth century B.C. and which may have been written by one of his followers. Half a century later, Aristotle takes up this parallel in his *Politics*, Book VII, chapter 6, and adds that "the race of the Greeks", combining the attributes of Nordic man, courageous but unorganized, and of the Orientals, clever but too subservient to despots, "remains free and preserves the best form of government". And he adds: "It could bring all the nations under its rule, if it were united in a single state."

2. Strabo, a Pontine Greek (born in 66 B.C. and died in the reign of Tiberius), left a description of the known world, from the Iberian peninsula to countries in Asia beyond the Taurus. He repeatedly emphasizes the *variety* of living conditions which makes for fruitful *exchanges* between the peoples of Europe.

3. *Géographie universelle*, by L. Mantelle and Malte Brun, Paris 1816. The passage quoted by Paul Valery is to be found in Variété I, La Crise de l'Esprit, Paris 1924.

4. These figures are necessarily inexact, and can only indicate orders of size. Estimates of China's present population vary between 480 and 750 millions, accord-

ing to the political leanings of the demographers. Western Europe (including Finland and Yugoslavia) has about 335 million inhabitants, and there are 95 millions in the satellite states of the USSR. According to whether what is known as "Russia in Europe", extending from the Urals to the Caspian Sea, is added to this total or not, the result is larger or smaller than the population of China. It is convenient to add the population of Pakistan to that of India (400 millions), making a total of about 500 millions.

5. Charles Morazé, *Essai sur l'Occident*, Armand Colin, Paris, 1950, p. 76: "The great enquiry of 1328 credits France with having the same population as that which Vauban estimated at the close of the reign of Louis XIV."

6. About 1850 the population of China was estimated at 400 millions, and world population at 1,200 millions; at that time therefore, China represented one-third of the world's population. Assuming a present-day population of 650 millions in China, this makes a little less than one quarter of the total world population, which is 2,800 millions. Estimates for the year 2,000 put the Chinese population at 1,100 millions and world population at 5,600 millions.

7. Karl Jaspers, *Nietzsche et le Christianisme*, French translation by Jeanne Hersche, Editions de Minuit, Paris 1949. See also my *Aventure Occidentale de l'Homme*, Albin Michel, Paris 1957, chap. VII, L'Exploration de la Matière.

8. Cf. André Varagnac, *Comment est née l'Europe?* (in La Table Ronde, no. 113, Paris 1957) and *L'Homme Avant L'Ecriture*, Armand Colin, Paris 1959, table p. 374. See also the classical works of V. Gordon Childe, especially

"The Dawn of European Civilisation" (French translation, Payot, Paris 1949).

9. On the etymology of Europe cf. my *Vingt-Huit Siècles d'Europe*, Payot, Paris 1961, pp. 28–33. The historic truth of the legend of the abduction of Europa has recently been confirmed yet again by the deciphering of some "linear A" inscriptions in Crete by British and American scholars; it is a Phoenecian language written in Greek characters.

10. Regarding the legend of Cadmus, see Robert Graves, *The Greek Myths*, 2 vols., Penguin Books, London 1955, I, pp. 194–7. On the settlement of the Phoenecians in Boeotia, cf. Victor Berard, La Résurrection d'Homère, pp. 190 and 191, Paris 1930.

11. Genesis 9, 20–7 and the whole of chapter 10, on which the Fathers based their speculations. There is a very detailed discussion of this in Juergen Fischer: *Oriens, Occidens, Europa, Begriff und Gedanke "Europa" in der spaeten Antike und im frueheren Mittelalter*, F. Steiner Verlag, Wiesbaden 1957.

12. Columbus's or (Colonist's) titles were given him in a letter written from Barcelona by Ferdinand and Isabella on 30 March 1493: "Don Cristobal" returned in triumph from the "Indies". On the origins of the Grand Admiral of the Ocean Sea, on scientific research by Portuguese, Italians and Germans which formed the basis for his calculations, and on the "fantastic biblical-cosmographic edifice" which he was to compose later on to explain his discoveries, see Salvador de Madariaga's admirable and scholarly "Christophe Colomb" (Calmann-Lévy, Paris 1952).

13. Some Irish landed in Iceland as early as 795. A hundred years later the Normans or Vikings, still pagans

themselves, found on this island, which they called Thule (Tyli) a Christian community which is described in the *Landnamabok* written about 1200. The first expedition from Scandinavia which was chronicled goes back to 870. It was formed by Norwegians fleeing from the tyranny of a local king, Harald the fair haired. From Iceland the Vikings went on to explore and colonise Greenland, where Eric the Red reigned at the close of the tenth century. From there they discovered first Labrador and then Nova Scotia, and finally the north of the United States, which they named "Vinland", vine-country; it was the Maine coast. A runic stone discovered in 1898 in Minnesota is evidence of the expedition made in 1362 by some Swedes and Norwegians on orders from the court of Norway "to find and bring back to Christendom the colonists from Greenland who had disappeared". (Report of the National Museum of Washington, quoted by Paul Herrmann, *L'Homme á la decouverte du Monde*, French translation Plon, Paris 1954).

II

THE SECRETS OF EUROPE'S VITALITY

II

THE SECRETS OF EUROPE'S VITALITY

I HAVE retraced the fabulous adventure of the inhabitants of the western cape of Asia, in which they extended their power to all the continents in succession from the Renaissance until the two world wars, and I have dealt with the withdrawal of which we are witnessing the last phases, bringing Europe back once more to the territorial limits which were hers in the fifteenth century. And I left you with the question: "Is this the end of the Adventure?"

I believe that any prognosis about Europe should be based on an examination of three factors which have a decisive influence on the future of the patient: her intrinsic vitality, her will to live, and lastly her function in the world, in other words her vocation.

Vitality, will, vocation. To deal first with vitality: what are Europe's long-term prospects, and what are the secrets of that unique vitality in the history of humanity which has sustained our worldwide adventure up to the present? Are these secrets of our expansion still alive and active?

Is Europe's centrality an illusion?

Let us begin by examining the geo-economic situation of our small continent up to the present point in the evolution of the world. We shall discover that this situation is *more central than ever*, however strange this statement may appear.

We have often been warned, since the beginning of the century, against the provincial illusion which would have us imagine Europe to be the World's centre. Toynbee recently repeated the warning. Undoubtedly such warnings are prompted by a healthy spirit, for collective vanity is just as reprehensible as individual pride and, like the latter often comes before destruction. But, as we know too well, ethics count for very little in history. Let us try to take a hard look at the facts, rather than yielding to that self-denigrating complex which is still the bane of too many western intellectuals. It is stupid and blameworthy to believe oneself to be the centre of the world *if in fact one is not*. But if it turns out that one is, it would be equally stupid and blameworthy to deny it simply for the sake of a quite hypocritical humility, which would be nothing more than a mask for inverted pride, transformed into masochism—a most unscientific attitude.

Let us then look at some facts which can be measured. At the close of the last war, in 1944 and 1945, some geographers and economists attached to the British and American air forces published some studies which have remained fairly confidential. To me the conclusions reached in these studies appear very striking. (Incidentally, the studies carried on and brought up to date work done by British and German geographers and published in 1906 and 1930). Here then is the starting point of these studies.[1]

The privileged hemisphere

Of all the infinite number of hemispheres which can be traced on our globe there is one, and only one, which contains both 94 per cent of the present population of the world and 98 per cent of the world's production —hence the title of *privileged hemisphere* given to it by geographers. Thus the other half of the world, seen from this viewpoint, contains only 6 per cent of its inhabitants and 2 per cent of its production, for it is occupied mainly by the oceans, the continent of Antarctica, Patagonia and Australia. Now here is the point I find so striking: the pole of this hemisphere falls in Europe, just south of Nantes according to the American authors—though the British place it nearer to London and the Germans to Berlin—but in any case on our continent. Thus, if one were to take a point above Nantes, far enough from the earth to be able to see the whole of the privileged hemisphere through a telescope, one would see nearly 19/20ths of humanity, whilst from the corresponding situation in the Antipodes only water and deserts would be visible, save for some traces of human activity at the fringes.

Here then is a measurable fact which depends neither on our pride nor our humility as Europeans, one which can be easily verified, the objective data for which can be read off our global atlases and economic maps pending the day when they are photographed by a man-made satellite: *Europe is actually the centre of the world*, the geometric centre and the natural crossroads of the main sea, and, above all, air routes by the aid of which the human race has become aware of its oneness in useful, practical ways.

What is the meaning of this fact, which quite evidently is not merely physical but also human, not only geographical but also cultural? It suggests a correspondence which cannot be fortuitous between Europe's position in the world and her special function.

Position and function of Europe

Of course, it is not just Europe's position at the centre of the inhabited world and of the sea routes connecting its parts, which has made her what she is; for she became Europe at a period—call it, for example, the Middle Ages—when the distribution of men and their production was quite different from what it has become in our era. On the contrary, it looks as if the privileged hemisphere was built up *starting from* Europe, and by the actions of Europeans. And here I come back to my original contention; it is Europe which made the world, in the sense that she discovered it, explored it, exploited it, awakened it and set it on the road to unity by creating first of all its network of exchanges and centres of production, and then the first worldwide institutions. Neither the Africans nor the Chinese nor the Hindus nor the Arabs could have conceived and planned anything even remotely resembling the League of Nations or the United Nations; nor have they in fact done so. These institutions were the fruit of international law which itself (as is too often forgotten) was created by Europeans from the sixteenth and seventeenth centuries onwards, beginning with maritime law, with Hugo Grotius and discussions about the souls of "savages", and with Francisco de Vitoria.[2]

So Europe's world function can be seen clearly,

almost diagrammatically, at the heart of the privileged hemisphere; and this is a crucial fact for anybody who sets out to weigh up the future of the West and of the European spirit.

In my first lecture I outlined those systole and diastole movements which form the rhythm of Europe's history on the world stage. To see now how these alternations were bound up with geographical facts, but above all with the action of the men who made Europe, let us leave our vantage point in the sky and progressively reduce our range of vision from that of overall survey to the study of human relations at ground level.

Bird's-eye view of Europe: Compartments

First we come down from 100 to 50 miles. Comparing the continents as a whole (either from the American satellite Tiros I or simply on a geographical globe marked in relief) we see that present-day Europe, cut off at the Russian steppes, would go into Asia about nine times, and into Africa about six times. But on the other hand, this small continent is the most complex of them all; it is the most deeply indented by the sea and the most variously divided by mountainous folds of medium height and rivers which can be easily crossed. It is made up of peninsulas and compartments, but they are neither too big nor too watertight; there are no endless plains, impassable mountain ranges or raging rivers cut by cataracts. The compartments all have their own individuality, but they also communicate with one another. It is worth remembering that in proportion to its surface area Europe has the longest coastline (4,500 miles more than Africa), more ports, the densest network of water communications (rivers and canals), the greatest concentration of towns and villages, and the most even spread of population. It is the only continent which is entirely free from deserts.

Bird's-eye view of Europe:
density of human labour

As we continue our descent towards this territory at the centre of the world, it will be instructive to compare some aerial photographs of approximately equal areas, say about six miles square, taken at an altitude of 10,000 feet over the Middle West or Brazil, China or Arabia, India or Black Africa and lastly Europe. The photograph of Europe will be recognized immediately; for nowhere else in the world will the landscape appear so intensively adapted to human life, cultivated, moulded, decorated and exploited by man's activity. There are lowlands won from the sea, rivers with their curves straightened by canals, tunnels for roads and railways, roads and bridges innumerable, and endless cultivation of fields. Take a magnifying glass and look at this photograph of a district—it might be in the Rhine or Moselle valleys, in Luxembourg, Belgium, or Switzerland: you can make out villages, small towns, and isolated farms, castles and factories, roads, railways and canals, forests and fields patterned with crops—traces of man and human labour everywhere, concentrated as nowhere else in the world.

And of all these ancient villages and towns in Europe you will not find any two which have exactly the same street plan. If they have something in common it is their complexity, or their knack of being different. Here we have the first hallmark of that paradoxical unity by which we can define Europe. It is a unity made up not of uniformity but on the contrary of variety of shapes and complexity of structures. Europe was born of its multitude of free towns and parishes, which fitted into the landscape and which used for its military, agricultural or commercial ends lands that to a large extent had once belonged to the Church. The nucleus might be a valley or a rocky outcrop, a river mouth or valley entrance, a confluence or a cross-roads, a ford or an agricultural centre—in other words a boundary, a centre or a passage; any of these natural features might serve as the focus for a nascent human community, whether village or town, once the original defensive stage, the era of central *Burg* and ramparts, had been outlived. In America towns arise as if by chance, along the routes opened up by the pioneers; they have little or no roots—they are on the move. These houses set among trees, spaced out along the highway, look like those covered wagons of the pioneers which pulled in at the end of the day's trek and then decided to stay put. In Asia the houses are crowded together in swarms. In Africa the huts are grouped in a circle in clearings, or strung out along river banks. In Europe alone does one see a network of deeply rooted communities, quite clearly individualized and yet amply interconnected, and federated regionally.

The original town square

Now we shall leave the silent skies and aerial photographs so curiously reminiscent of abstract art, and land on the soil of Europe, amid the human bustle of the central square of a small town. Once here, we have only to look about us to see the whole secret in microcosm. For around this square you will see the church and the town hall, probably the school and the cafes and the market and the traffic. From this very square, typical in its ordinariness, a scholar from Mars or Venus would be able to deduce without too much error the essential structures of our civilization.

A religious service, a meeting of the local council, a school lesson, talk around a pub table, or a walk among the market stalls would reveal to him some of the secrets (very obvious to us) of the vitality of Europe; secrets such as shared spiritual values, the rule of law, the tacit respect accorded by all citizens to public institutions, public education, free expression of opinion (preferably argumentative and subversive) and division of labour —vitality ordered in freedom, a balanced mass of interacting tensions.

Morphology of Europe

So now let us sketch a portrait of Europe as she can be *seen* by any one of us. This will not be a portrait based on abstract definitions and intellectual analyses of principles and doctrines; for it would always be easy to say that these are scarcely ever put into practice, that they describe an ideal Europe which one refuses to recognize, the Europe of the others—the other school, the other party. Instead we shall start from those visible, tangible realities which surround us in our daily lives. We shall try to draw a morphological rather than a philosophical sketch of Europe. I believe this is a somewhat novel approach, and I do not underestimate the difficulties.

But perhaps it may be a source of fruitful ideas to some young sociologists who may wish to carry it farther; it might suggest a new method of education in civics based on photographs and films, and prompting many revealing comparisons with things as they are on other continents. Let us, then, try to reconstruct Europe with the town or village square as our starting point.

Our towns and villages did not rise round squares which had been laid out in readiness. They grew up around a citadel, a fortress defending a strategic point. Nevertheless, it is really the creation of the Square in the *faubourgs—fori burgus*, places outside the original defensive fortress—which gave visible proof that Europeans had really achieved a communal life, which is the foundation of our civilization. Truly, we feel, squares such as these were built neither by the amorphous masses nor by militarized masses, neither by the crowd nor the despot; they are laid out to serve practical, communal needs. Dictatorships only build geometrically; they line up bureaucratic facades around an empty circle or a rectangle reminiscent of tedious parades. By contrast, the central Squares in our towns and villages are seldom regular in shape—except those built in periods of civic decline, strict state control and tyranny. In spite of its name, a square in Britain disdains right-angles as much as the Palio at Sienna, the Piazza della Signoria at Florence or the Forum at Rome itself, which is the common ancestor of our *places*, *Plätze*, *plazas*, *praças*, *piazze*, or *Pleins*, according to the country. As for the Forum's own ancestor, that was the *agora* of the Greeks, where western civic consciousness was born.

43

Town Hall and Parliaments

Whether or not the Town Hall (hotel de ville, municipio, Rathaus, mairie) is situated on the square—and it usually is—its original purpose is bound up with the square. The *parties* which determine the composition of the city council were formed first of all in the *agora*, then in the forum of Republican Rome, and still later in the squares of the towns and cities of the Middle Ages. Sunlight and shadow move with the passing hours—from church side to school side, from the municipal buildings round to the café. With the market in the centre, it is the main centre for the exchange of goods and gossip from the surrounding district, and rumours and influences from afar. It is this life of the market square which, in essence, reappears in that of the councils and parliaments which are characteristic of Europe. (The last surviving image of this very specific origin of parliaments is found to-day in the *Landsgemeinde* of the small Swiss cantons, forming the Ring on the main square.)

The café and the Press

All democracy, in the European meaning of the word, rests upon freedom of discussion, free party activity and freedom for the opposition which may tomorrow be the majority. In modern Europe, however, parties, opinion and especially opposition, find their expression in the press; and right from the start the press has been closely connected with that other essential feature of any square worthy of the name—the *café*. That is where news is first talked about, often written, and certainly read. Huguenot refugees met in cafés in Holland and created the famous French language gazettes which were distributed throughout the whole of Europe despite the censorship of an absolute government, thus paving the way for the Enlightenment and the French Revolution. It was in English taverns that the editorials of the journal edited single-handed by Daniel Defoe were read aloud, from 1704 to 1713. It was in the coffee-houses too that Addison's *Spectator* tried to bring philosophy, once the preserve of the educated few, to the common man. So let us not omit from our picture of the town square the newspaper stall, purveyor of news from the outside world, between the café and the market.[3]

Church and choir

Opposite the town hall is the *church*. In the Greek *agora* it was the temple, in the Roman forum it was the altar, and now it is the Christian church or *ecclesia* (which meant *assembly* not temple); these represent the other pole of the city, that of basic beliefs held in common which must transcend party differences, ambitions and the doctrines of the moment. Confining one's judgement strictly to outward manifestations, as I intend to do just now, what goes on in this church which has never been known in the East? The priest or minister speaks and intones, the people respond, and the choir sings. And this choir is made up of voices which are different, yet united by the laws of harmony, rhythm and prosody. Each voice makes itself heard in its own way, freely and enthusiastically and, whilst keeping to its own distinct part, contributes to the final

45

hosanna in which all voices are one. Individual salva-
tion but a communal service; and the music sung in
church also reveals the essentially polyphonic and dialectical structure which defines Europe, both in her
greatness and her downfall.[4]

It would be tempting to take this as a starting point
for a reconstitution of the whole philosophy of the
person, that is to say of the individual at once autonomous
and committed—bound up with the community . . .
But this would be to stray from my subject. I will only
point out that it could be done almost as well by taking
the school, also found on the square, as a starting point.

School initiation and initiative

Education was a function of the Church in the Middle
Ages; then, at the Renaissance, from the Reformation
and the Orders of the church. Nowadays its teachers,
paid by the town hall or its equivalent, often give more
attention to the controversies of the café than to the
objurgations of the bishop. Thus another tension is
produced. But the function of the school has not
changed; on the one hand it must pass on the store of
knowledge together with respect for the values of the
community, and on the other hand it must awaken the
critical sense and individual judgement. To educate is
e-ducere, to lead out. To lead the individual, but lead
him to self-discovery just as much as to the discovery
of the great common heritage of which the City is the
result, which sustains it and which must be criticized
to be kept alive—but criticized by standards taught in
the school . . . The function of the school in the city,
then, may be summed up in the two words *initiation* and

initiative, indicating the two poles of our education. (Until quite modern times, *initiating* education was almost the only kind known in the Orient and the traditional cultures.)

The Market

As for the *market*, which occupies the centre of the square, where the products of the country supply the needs of the town, and where living expression is given to the law of supply and demand, it has been the symbolic description of the whole economy of Europe right up to the present day. And the ascendancy of this word continued even after the *port* (root of the verbs to import and export) had become more important to trade than the country market. For this is where the conflicting yet mutual interests of producer and consumer collide, where the bargaining takes place according to traditional rules, where new methods and old customs, local conditions and collective requirements meet, forces whose constant play determines the dynamic synthesis at any given moment.

Thus the consideration of the typical *buildings* and the main *functions* of which the square is composed enable us to feel, almost to see, the original pulsation of the energies which formed Europe. Within each of the spheres described—spiritual and civic, educational and economic—we have encountered analogous pairs of creative tensions, of necessary opposites, each of which appears at one and the same time paradoxical and yet completely valid. Added to this there are the numerous tensions, not only between the institutions themselves, but also between the township or local community (the

47

result of their local synthesis) and the region, then between the region and the nation, the nation and Europe, Europe and the world. In essence, these all relate to the tension between the *particular* in all its forms, even national, and the *universal* with all its claims, even though represented by the revolt of an individual genius or saint against a whole city for the sake of principles on which he will not compromise.

Our history is made of pluralism
and tensions

Defining Europe, then, by its social forms, we see that it is *pluralist* in principle, not unitary as were the great traditional, static civilizations of Asia, and of pre-Columbian America, and as the totalitarian regimes of our time wish to be. It is a civilization based on antagonisms, on ceaselessly renewed conflicts; a civilization of discussion and debate, whose overmastering passion seems to be constantly to re-examine the natural universe and human relationships, Destiny and the meaning of life.

When one of these conflicting realities—liberty or authority, local autonomy or centralization, innovation or tradition, individualism or social discipline, etc., aims at taking over completely and destroying the other for the sake of order and simplicity or of so-called total and unitary doctrine, the result is war, revolution, massacre and explosions of anarchy followed by dictatorships—a more intense, violent and polemical *history**
than is related in the chronicles of any other area of the world. When these antagonisms are resolved by a prac-

* There is a play upon the word *histoire*, which also means "trouble".

tical compromise, embodied in an institution or brought about by a method which overcomes the tension without suppressing it, thus avoiding both a depressing monotone and an unbearable discord, it is then that the most typical *creations* of European culture appear, not only in the arts but also in Society. One could say that they were based on the same principles as choral music, on the harmony of complementary sounds or on the calculated dissonance that points to a "resolution" in the future. This has been the history of the local government unit (town or commune), of the federation, parliament and the bi-cameral system, of trade unions and co-operatives; it has been true of education itself, as we have seen; lastly it has been true of the idea of progress.

It is evident that in so far as this immense complex of tensions is not too much debilitated or devastated by wars, dictatorships and inward-looking nationalism (all of which short-circuit these energies), in so far as even part of the potential accumulated by these tensions really develops, it acts as the centre of an irresistible expansion of energy. That is the secret of Europe's dynamism, and of the periods of worldwide diastole of our civilization.

Sounding the organs of
European society

Are we on the threshold of such a period? Or on the contrary is Europe in such a bad state of health as many of our intellectuals claim? More seriously, will not the triumph of technology very soon iron out our most fruitful diversities and impose upon our continent and its peoples an anonymous uniformity, comparable to the conventional idea of the average film producer, whether Russian or American? I suggest that by listening to the main organs of the City, those traditional institutions of which our symbolic buildings, grouped around the square, are the outward expression, we could obtain the material for a reasoned reply to this question—one which is too often and too lightly raised merely to foster reactionary or progressive prejudice. How are they adapting themselves to the technical era? Here I must limit myself to a few brief indications, purely factual or comparative.

Health of the Church

First of all the *churches*, since they are the oldest. In most of our villages the single church is usually three-quarters empty, whereas in America they are crowded every Sunday and on an average one would find four or five of them in a rural community of between 2,000 and 3,000 inhabitants. To a greater extent than with us, the church has remained the centre of the social life of a village, with an important place in political and civic life. But perhaps this is at the expense of discipline in doctrine and in the spiritual life which Europe has been able better to maintain in opposition to the State and passing fashions. Americans are well aware of this, and consequently their pastors and priests are increasingly learning from our theologians. The three names which dominate present-day religious thought in America are Jacques Maritain, Paul Tillich and Karl Barth, a Frenchman, a German and a Swiss, three names which in Europe are closely linked with an undeniable resurgence of intellectual vitality in the churches. There is another sign, which you may think purely external but which seems to me revealing: in the land of the skyscraper they continue to build imitation Gothic churches, and even cathedrals which are composite copies of our Mediaeval basilicas, whereas all over Europe churches are being built of glass and reinforced concrete, and decorated by the most modern painters. They incorporate all the discoveries of the technological age, yet for all that serve their traditional purpose—to better effect, in fact, than the miserable and gloomy buildings put up in the nineteenth century.

But undoubtedly the general movement towards *ecumenicalism* is the most striking symptom of a spiritual rebirth within the churches. In the World Council of Churches, of which nearly all the Protestant, Anglican and Orthodox churches are members; in the movement within Roman Catholicism symbolized by the Ecumenical Council convened by Pope John XXIII; in intercommunion agreements made between Lutherans, Anglicans, Old Catholics and Orthodox; in the numerous fusions between Protestant denominations in Europe, the United States and India; in the innumerable meetings between theologians of the great Christian confessions, which have been taking place for decades with the permission, at least, of their ecclesiastical hierarchies, we are witnessing in this generation a phenomenon of *Christian reunion* which reverses the course of religious history for the last thousand years and more. Liturgical developments among Protestants, bible study among Catholics, a new social awareness among both and among the Orthodox, all these things combine to bring the confessions closer not only to one another but to their common source of inspiration. The worldwide scope of this phenomenon, which began in Europe, bears witness to a fresh lease of life for the Church as a force in history.

Health of Education

Now for a look at the educational system, the *schools*. They were said to be very much behind the times, too much bound by tradition, and there is still some justification for this criticism. But I notice that in America they are rediscovering the virtues of a non-specialized culture and of the humanities; they now favour a more disciplined, even authoritarian, pedagogy. Consequently they are looking to Europe in their search for a system that will balance the immediate preoccupation with training scientists and technicians, however relatively, with the long-term strategy of producing competent thinkers. Even the Soviet Union, where during the Stalinist period everything else was sacrificed to the teaching of technical subjects, is now admitting general studies again and, to that extent at least, is aligning itself with our European approach.[6]

Health of civic life

Let us turn now to the *town hall*, symbol of the local community, which is the concrete framework of civic life. In all our Western countries it has somehow or other survived more than a century of state encroachment and of systematic centralization. It might be thought that the technical age, in which large-scale planning is the order of the day, would have dealt it a mortal blow. Nothing of the sort has happened. Indeed,

the best specialists on the subject maintain that in the
interests both of good practice and of the health
of the technical economy itself, some reorganization
of industry is needed as well as more decentraliza-
tion of production leading to full utilization, through
the local authorities, of the resources of development
areas within the national territories. Even in the most
centralized countries, such as France, the tendency
towards a restoration of local government powers is
gathering strength every year. The continent-wide
activity of the *Conseil des Communes d'Europe* and the
Union des Villes et des Pouvoirs Locaux, both formed since
the last war, far from being a rearguard action against
state powers, is at the forefront of a renewal of municipal
autonomy.[7]

Prosperity of the market

As for the market which occupies the middle of the
square, it is obviously enjoying unprecedented prosperity in all our countries, whether one thinks of the
Common Market of the Six or of the economies of the
neutral countries.

. . . and of the press

Coming lastly to the *press* and to the *café* which was its
midwife if not its progenitor, I shall content myself with
one elementary observation. The total absence of a free
press in the Soviet Union and the lack of literary and
political "coffee houses" in the United States are not
simply matters for regret to some travellers from
Europe, annoyed at being unable to engage in their

favourite pastime of intellectual dissent. The prosperity of the free press and the reputation enjoyed by these cafés in our larger towns where talkers and thinkers foregather—two facts unequal in importance but both very typical of our Europe—are still unmistakeable signs of a culture which is modern and rooted in social life, which can criticize and therefore lead to renewal.

Europe and culture

To sum up, then, the secret of Europe is *culture* in the wider meaning of the term—*what man does with nature.* Apart from her culture, Europe is just a promontory of Asia, with few natural resources and is, I repeat, less thickly populated than India or China. But this promontory and its inhabitants, wrought upon, tormented and fertilized for centuries by religious ferment and doctrine, by philosophic forms of thought, and by an urge to intellectual adventure which gave birth to science and technology, a flowering of the arts and of social life and institutions, together with unprecedented economic power—that is Europe, the Europe that made the world. Shorn of her culture Europe would amount to very little.

This definition recalls to my mind the most famous equation of this century, that of Einstein: $E = mc^2$, where E means energy, m mass and c the speed of light. I shall transpose it term by term, Europe of course being E, m the continent's small physical mass, and c its culture.

In these terms, this is what $E = mc^2$ means: Europe is equal to a promontory of Asia multiplied by intensive culture (c^2). (I hasten to add—just in case—that this is not intended as a pseudo-mathematical *proof*, simply an *illustration*).

It is this remarkable concentration of pluralist institutions in tension, and this perpetual and overt struggle between tradition and innovation, which have rendered Europe capable of *assimilating* technical advance rather better than some other parts of the world.

A crowded canvas

America and Russia with their huge, thinly-peopled plains, were virgin territory offering very few obstacles to the development of technological civilization. But in Europe its environment was already honey-combed with venerated principles and guaranteed rights, beset with a tangle of age-old customs of workers and peasants, of legal or fiscal subtleties, of insurrections and demands by the people, which reduced its momentum and compelled it little by little to take account of its human environment and not to behave like a bull in a china shop or a bulldozer in an orchard. True, these brakes and dams did not always act in time, and the social conscience of the ruling classes was slow to awaken. The first industrial revolution, based on coal, created not only the grimy, soulless pattern of the suburbs around our capitals; it also created the proletariat, subjecting a whole class of human beings to machines which were still very primitive and making the workman, as Marx put it, "the living appendage of a dead machine", compelling him to work fifteen hours a day under inhuman conditions both from the hygienic and moral point of view. This first technical explosion did far more harm to our species than the nuclear explosions which appal us to-day. But it was not reported in the press, and its effects were spread out over a century.

From the black age to the white age

But by developing techniques through science and then humanizing them through social legislation, by passing from the black age of coal, mines and smoky factories to the clean, white age of electricity, air travel and glass-walled factories in green surroundings, Europe did more than bring technology closer to its true goal, which is to set man free from menial work. She was the first to become aware of the social, moral, educational and spiritual problems henceforth confronting mankind as a result of the technology and science which owed their origins to her. It was her leading thinkers that first formulated the problem of the essential balance between tradition and innovation which is the basic problem of our age; and she alone brings to its solution the background of age-long experience.

Europe's way: continuity and innovation

For Africa, Asia and the Arab world know only tradition, and therefore innovation overtakes them like a tempest. America, on the other hand, has had no Middle Ages: men there have less ballast from the past, and are more easily carried away by surface currents. Americans do indeed come from Europe, and in that sense our Middle Ages are also theirs. But we have among us, at the heart of our towns, daily and *familiar* reminders of our past—Roman ruins, alleys, and cathedrals, classical and baroque palaces; they do not have these things. And Russia did not experience the Renaissance and the Reformation; therefore men there are less ready to live out their own individual adventure, and are more easily dominated by the established power of the collective. A certain human equilibrium between collective disciplines and individual liberties, between continuity and innovation, between the reassuring weight of traditions and the urge to risk everything for adventure, a certain sense of identity amid changes—this perhaps is the last secret which Europe, among the nations, possesses.

I conclude from all this that an examination of the organs and metabolism of the patient called Europe reveals that she has very sound reasons for feeling a lot better than she is said to be, and better than she often thinks she is.

But does she have the *will* to live?

By that I mean, will Europe be able to rally its life force in time to meet not only its own problems in education, political and social life, but also the global tasks newly laid upon it by the spread of its own civilization and its own ideals?

A monument to the absurdity of history

Lastly, will it be able to avert those terrible threats to its mental health and physical existence symbolized in the village square, by one more monument which I have not yet mentioned; a monument that reminds us of all the unreason of history as well as the concept of a *national* as opposed to Christian demand for limitless devotion that exists in many countries not far from Switzerland: the memorials to the dead of two world wars?

NOTES ON CHAPTER II

1. The first studies on the "privileged hemisphere" were made as far back as 1906 by Philipson and Neumann in Germany and Mackinder in England. In 1930 the distinguished English geographer published a more thorough study. Lastly, Parker van Zandt in the USA. (in 1944) and H. Taylor (in 1945) for the Royal Air Force, studied the problem from the point of view of air communications. There is a good map of the privileged hemisphere in Parker van Zandt's *Strategy of an Air Age*, The Brookings Institution, Washington DC, 1944.

2. Bartolomeo de Las Casas, the evangelist of the Indians, spoke up for them before the King and the son of Columbus from 1519 onwards. His *Brevissima relacion de la destruccion de las Indias*, published at Seville in 1552, is the first recorded indictment of colonialism and founded a long tradition which has persisted up to the present—a European tradition, be it noted. The famous monk Francisco de Vitoria in his *De Indis*, 1532, documented the right of the Indians to possess their land, and assigned to Spaniards only the right of travelling to the Indies for the purpose of converting the heathen there. Another Spanish monk, the Jesuit Francisco Suarez (1548-1617) and the liberal Calvinist Hugo Grotius (1583-1645), though starting from very different premises, are considered with Vitoria to be the founders of the Western *jus gentium*.

3. The first picture booklets (the illustrated journals of the age) were made by Albert Dürer (1471-1528). He did the engraving, printing and sub-titling himself, and his wife went and sold them in the *town square*, at the *market* and in *taverns*.

4. In India there are no community ceremonies, apart from the great processions. But there are little shrines in their hundreds of thousands were a single man or woman stands praying before a tiny idol.

5. Cf. my essay entitled *The Golden Rule* (Bulletin du Centre Europeen de la Culture, Noc. 3, 8th year, 1961), containing the substance of a lecture given as Professor of Pedagogy at the Humanities School of Geneva University.

6. For a more thorough treatment of this vitally important point, the reader is referred to the study mentioned in note 5. As regards the USSR my authority was the research done at Harvard by Prof. Nicolas de Witt, in which the extreme degree of specialization reached by 1950-55 was described. Since that time the Harvard Institute of Sovietic Studies has been able to follow and publicize the progress of the evolution in Russia towards the re-establishment of general studies. See also on this subject the comparative study of primary and secondary education in the USA and the USSR by Prof. Arthur S. Trace: *What Ivan knows that Sammy doesn't*, Random House, New York 1961. This work is more polemical (against the United States) but is well documented.

7. *L'Union des Villes et des Pouvoirs Locaux*, which has its headquarters at The Hague, has organized several congresses of mayors and issued some important publications on the position with regard to the problems facing

municipalities in our countries, particularly: *Die Grosse Stadt und die Kleine Gemeinde* (Big City and Small Community), Congress of Vienna June 1953, and the *Communes d'Europe* (Local Government Units in Europe) by the ministers Pierre Wigny (Belgium) and H.-J von Merkatz (Federal Republic), The Hague, 1955.

The *Conseil des Communes d'Europe*, which has a more pronounced federalist outlook, was founded in Geneva in 1951 and embraces about 40,000 local government authorities. Its headquarters are at Paris and the moving spirits are Frenchmen (Messieurs J. Chaban-Delmas, mayor of Bordeaux, and G. Deferre, mayor of Marseilles, in particular). It publishes a review entitled "Communes d'Europe". A great many towns in Europe have "paired up" under the auspices of the CCE, giving rise to demonstrations of European solidarity by their inhabitants.

Lastly a *Commission Européenne des Pouvoirs locaux* (European Commission of Local Authorities) was set up at the Council of Europe in Strasbourg.

III

EUROPE UNITES

EUROPE UNITES

TAKEN ONE by one, the vital organs of our society appear to me to be in quite good condition. It remains to discover whether the subject of our enquiry, Europe, still possesses a sufficient will to live to be able to fulfil the new functions which from now on are allotted to it in the world. I shall now endeavour to show that in practice, Europe's will to live means her *will to unite.*

From diversity to division

These two things are not necessarily identical. Indeed, there might seem to be a contradiction between giving Europe a clean bill of health and saying that she needs to unite. For if all is well, why do we need to unite? Nations feel this need only at times of crisis, as a reaction against internal ills or against a peril from outside. Union is not an end in itself; it is a means to the end of survival, or of attaining a better life. It is even, in practical terms, a cure. But to speak of a cure is to acknowledge a disease. So what is this illness which afflicts Europe despite her organic soundness? I believe that it is of psychic origin.

Its overall effect is to transform our living, vital *diversities* into rigid, morbid *divisions*; political in origin they spread to the economic field and finally attack the common basis of our diversities—the unity of our traditional, creative culture. The short name for this sickness is *nationalism*, which is the claim by states to absolute sovereignty, in which they enclose their economy and even their culture but not, alas, always their armies. The fact that Europe has come close to destroying herself twice within the present century must be laid at the door of extreme nationalism. And it is this very disease, which we have planted on many continents formerly colonised by us, that causes the fevers and the paroxysms of hate against Europe from which so many emergent countries in Africa, the Arab world and Asia have suffered during the last few years.

Thus I believe that if we can show that the will to unite exists it will prove that Europe once more has the will to live; for it would stem from the desire to overcome our nationalist divisions, and thereby *restore that healthy play to our diversities which is the sign of normality.* The will to unite will be a sign of renewed health in the body of Europe in so far as it aims at federating our differences, not ironing them out or making life uniform throughout the continent. *That* could be done by allowing technology to proliferate without checking it. The will to unite will be healthy if it tends to eliminate the virus of nationalism, not to offer it greater scope by creating a continent transformed into a super-nation and saddled with a super-nationalism.

Three conceptions of union

I shall deal straight away with these definitions of unity, thus making clear my own position in the context of the discussion now going on about Europe. For there is a struggle between two extreme and opposite views

64

on this matter. One has been known for some little time as "L'Europe des patries", or Europe made up of separate fatherlands (a fundamentally incorrect expression, by the way). This school would like to stick to an alliance of national states all keeping their sovereignty intact. It is the minimal position. The other, which can be broadly described as that of the Common Market, wishes to unify the nations on the basis of full economic integration. That is the maximal position. The former places its main emphasis on the points of difference, the latter on unity. My belief is that the only unity which is compatible with the genius of Europe itself, with its past, with its realities and its present vocation, is *unity in diversity*, a strong yet flexible union of which Switzerland has perfected the prototype: and that means federalism.

A discussion of the merits of these three schools of thought—that of alliances, that of integration and that of federation—would be outside the scope of this book, which is not about politics.

Nevertheless, I think it is essential to trace the origins of these three lines of thought, and to discover the source of the discussion about the union of Europe which has been in full spate for several years in the press and at meetings all over the continent. (It has even crossed the channel to Britain, and recently reached the United States).

For it is impossible to understand what is at stake in this great contemporary discussion, or its themes, without first seeing them against the background of our history. It is taking place at what seems to be the end of long evolution which has shaped the thought, feelings and reflexes of Europeans, and which therefore determines whether they are instinctively repelled by, or enthusiastically support, the various solutions offered.

The idea of unifying or federating Europe was not born yesterday. To be exact, even on the evidence of existing documents, it goes back to the beginning of the fourteenth century. Moreover, the small extent to which its themes have changed over the centuries is very striking. What is happening before our eyes, very imperfectly as yet, it is true—is what was vainly advocated exactly six and a half centuries ago by visionary poets and great philosophers, as well as by some hard-headed politicians, from Dante through Goethe to Victor Hugo, from Sully through Montesquieu, Rousseau and Saint-Simon to Churchill, and from Leibnitz through Kant to Nietzsche.

Four themes of unity

For all these men, and for hundreds of others whom I have quoted and about whom I have written in a recent work entitled *Twenty-eight centuries of Europe*[1] there were ultimately four great, simple reasons why it was imperative for Europe to unite. These themes are nearly always all present, although one or another of them may be more dominant according to the age and the school of thought. Here then are those four constant themes.

First of all, *peace*, which must be guaranteed to our peoples, torn by the internecine wars in Europe; peace through an authority higher than nations and princes, an authority which suppresses any attempt at hegemony. This was the dominant theme throughout the Middle Ages.

Next, the re-establishment of a *spiritual community sup-*

ported by a common legal framework. Already present in Dante, this theme comes to the fore after the Reformation and is prominent all through the period of absolutism in which sovereign States were formed, from the sixteenth to the eighteenth century.

Lastly, *the prosperity of all,* which has to be organized on the continental scale, not at State level. This theme is characteristic of the modern period, from Saint-Simon and Bentham around 1800 up to the Common Market in our time.

The theme of a *threat from outside,* or of *common defence,* which many modern authors consider to be essential in awakening a sense of the need for unity, has often been invoked over the centuries. Until the eighteenth century the Turks filled the role of bogeyman; then in the nineteenth century it was the turn of the Russians and of the Yellow Peril; now it is the Two Super-Powers who have the Bomb. But in fact this fear motive is incidental, and has not been a driving force in our history. Whether the adversary be Turkish or Soviet it is a welcome pretext inasmuch as it allows the positive thesis which is being defended—peace, spiritual community or prosperity— to be dramatized. It is pre-eminently a means of persuading Princes, and later on public opinion, to act.

Broadly speaking, union is desired in order to *overcome the permanent state of anarchy* resulting from the claims of nations and states to absolute sovereignty, and their rejection of any common authority above their interests or ambitions, which they call their rights.

As to the theme of *imperialism*—"Let us march out *together* and conquer the world"—I find no mention of it in any plan or thesis, with the sole exception of those of the Jacobins. Certainly it inspired first Napoleon and

67

then Hitler in their brief and unsuccessful attempts to unify Europe by force, each of which lasted about a dozen years. But the prophets and advocates of federal union have always maintained that one of the outstanding effects of union would be to remove any temptation to imperialism or even colonialism.

These four main themes (peace, spiritual community, prosperity, and defence), I repeat, are all to be found in the thinking of all the advocates of unity whom I shall name, but the emphasis differs according to the epoch: this points to an evolution of themes or motives observable over the centuries, which it is interesting to retrace.

I shall therefore pass rapidly in review the great names which stand out as landmarks in this evolution, and the main schemes of unity which illustrate its various stages.

Dante

The first two date from the years 1306 and 1308. One is Dante's *De Monarchia*, and the other was the work of Pierre DuBois, a counsellor of Philip the Fair. Both were reacting against the growing anarchy caused in Europe by the quarrels between the Empire and the Church, the princes, the communes and the innumerable regional or, in the case of the king of France, even national sovereignties (the latter entering the conflict between the Pope and the Emperor like a third robber baron).

Dante's idea was a simple one; he wanted to see the establishment of a universal monarchy which, quite logically, would be sole judge in quarrels arising between princes who would be "independent and equal", and hence without powers over one another. Each of these would be master in his own lands, and each kingdom or town would retain its own "different laws", adapted to its customs; but on "common points affecting all men" the human species would be governed by a single monarch and "turned towards peace by a single law". Thus peace would once more come to Europe, which Dante declared to be "sick in its two intellects and in its sensibility", and which he described as "a many-headed monster dissipating itself in conflicting efforts". It would be an imperial peace, and Dante described it as the "fulness of times" predicted by St. Paul.[2]

Pierre DuBois

This sublime utopia of the poet, holding up the vision of a goal which though unattainable, was to haunt men's minds for centuries, had its counterpart in the down-to-earth empiricism of the Norman lawyer Pierre DuBois. He asked the following practical question: "If cities and princes recognize no higher power in this world, and if they are in conflict, before whom are they to state their case?" And DuBois answered: not before the universal monarch, but before a European tribunal. This tribunal of arbitration, composed of three prelates and three "wise and experienced" laymen, would be armed with sanctions. A country refusing to submit would be surrounded, isolated, and reduced by starvation; as for individual disturbers of the peace, they would be deported: they would be sent to fight against the Turks in the Holy Land, like a sort of Foreign Legion, rather than being allowed to continue bringing fire and blood to the "Christian Republic" (for "Christian" read "European").[3]

Needless to say, this plan received about as little attention as Dante's utopia. Not that it lacked realism; on the contrary, as one commentator wrote: "He was too much of a realist for his generation, which had very little realism."

This was the refrain with which all proposals for peace, from that day to this, were to be met. It took the atomic bomb finally to convince the nations and their rulers that it might be more realistic to help one another than to kill one another, and that therefore those who put forward plans for peace are not necessarily all soft dreamers or dangerous lunatics.

King George Podiebrad

Nevertheless, Pierre DuBois' idea was destined to survive. A hundred and fifty years later, in 1462, a poor Hussite of gentle birth, George Podiebrad, who had come to the throne of Bohemia, took up the torch. He put forward to the Christian princes and to the Pope a *Treaty of Alliance* which was, in fact, a plan for federation;[5] for, whilst guaranteeing the autonomy of the member states, it expressly limited their sovereignties. It involved the setting up of an Assembly, whose first meeting place was to have been Basle, of a Court of Justice, of a set of international rules for arbitration, of a common armed force and a common budget. All this is clearly much more progressive and modern than a plan which was to be proposed exactly five hundred years later called "L'Europe des patries", a plan that would be a reversion to a Europe composed of sovereign states, an alliance with a paradox at its heart and which it is to be feared, would be no easier to set up than a Friendly Society composed of misanthropists.

Podiebrad's plan was turned down by Louis XI, King of France, and by Pope Pius II, and nothing further was done about it. And yet this pope was none other than the great Aeneas Silvius Piccolomini, who at that very time was vainly trying to organize a new crusade, (for Byzantium had just fallen into the hands of the Turks), and who had been the first to speak of Europe as though it were a common fatherland, in his memorable letter to Mahomet II: "Now", he wrote "it is in *Europe itself, that is to say in our own fatherland,* in our own house, that we are being attacked and killed." [6]

Two centuries passed, and the face of Europe had changed. The great Discoveries, the Reformation and the establishment of states in the modern meaning of the word had caused great upheavals, and in particular the Thirty Years War. The time had come to re-think the relations between nations, that is to say between princes.

Efforts to restore order

Four plans on the grand scale contributed to this effort to restore order which was the keynote of the seventeenth century. All four vigorously emphasize Europe's federal vocation and the deep anxiety felt by the men of that age about the absolutist claims of states. All four were the product of minds which were deeply religious and therefore "ecumenical" in to-day's usage of the word, which implies the drawing closer together of the Christian confessions. Thus spiritual community, as well as peace, was one of the main inspirations of these plans. Lastly, all four passed unregarded by their contemporaries and yet survive in human memory long after the "realist" treaties of the period, which were soon effaced by history. To this day they have not ceased to influence the thinking of the creators of European institutions.

In chronological order, these four plans are: the *Nouveau Cynée* of Emeric Cruce, a Parisian monk, in 1623; Sully's *Grand Design* in 1638 (he was a Huguenot minister of Henry IV); the *Universal Dream* of Amos Comenius, a Moravian bishop, in 1645; and the *Essay on the present and future of Peace in Europe* by William Penn, the English Quaker and founder of a state in America, in 1692. There was a fifth at the beginning of the eighteenth century, the *Project of Perpetual Peace,* by the notorious Abbe de Saint-Pierre, in 1712.

To be frank, these plans were no great improvement on that of Podiebrad, though an examination of the facts compels their authors to repeat his main points. All of them propose a judicial tribunal which is above the states—or as we should say, supranational; they propose an Assembly, or Council of Europe; economic action on a continent-wide scale; and a common army in place of the armies of the Princes.

I shall therefore confine myself to mentioning any original or picturesque features of the various plans.

Emeric Cruce

Undoubtedly the most modern of these plans is the one which appeared first and of which least was heard, that of Emeric Cruce. All we know about him is that he was an obscure "teacher monk" in a college in Paris.[7] Three of his distinctive proposals are most astonishing considering the time when they were made: first, to include the Turks in the federation of Europe, which is rather like asking Soviet Russia to-day to join the Common Market, or even NATO; secondly, to end the wars of religion on the ground that the object of all religions is the same, namely the worship of God, and that their ceremonies are therefore of equal worth; "Only a narrow-minded person" he wrote, "believes that everyone ought to live as he does, or imagines only his own customs to be right, like those naive Athenians who thought their moon was brighter than that in any other country"; and third, to replace military training by educating the people in the sciences and manual skills, and to work out a scheme of great public works on the European scale, such as canals "joining the two seas", the reclamation of waste land, standardization of weights and measures, a common currency and the abolition of customs and tolls.

For all its astonishing richness, this plan was not followed up. But Leibnitz, another good European with an ecumenical outlook, was to read it later and make use of it.

Sully's "Grand Design"

The "Grand Design" which the Duc de Sully pretends to ascribe to King Henry IV of France was less original but much more widely known. It is constantly quoted and never read, with good reason. In reality it started off as a purely political scheme for a supranational pact between Protestant and Catholic princes against the house of Habsburg; but its substance is thinly spread through the thousands of pages of the *Memoires des sages et royales aeconomies*,[8] written long after the king's death by four secretaries who address the duke in the second person plural and thus recount his own life to him. In so far as it can be reconstituted, the plan provides for provincial councils and a General Council of Europe, limiting state sovereignty and guaranteeing freedom of trade. Its historical merit is that of having linked the prestige of a king to a high sounding title, "the Grand Design", which was to be repeated and invoked by innumerable advocates of unity, from William Penn and the abbe de Saint-Pierre to Churchill.

Comenius

Comenius[9] was the founder of modern pedagogy, the visionary forerunner of the ecumenical movement and of the worldwide federation. We shall single out from his *Universal Dream* the imposing scheme for a triple tribunal placed above individual states, and composed of the learned ones or "Council of Light" ecclesiastics or "Consistory", and politicians or statesmen the "Court of Justice". And we quote this memorable sentence "The light must be taken to other peoples in the name of our fatherland of Europe; that is why we must first of all unite among ourselves; for we Europeans must be looked upon as travellers who have all embarked on one and the same vessel." (May I remind you that this was written more than three hundred years ago).

William Penn

From the *Essay* by William Penn[10], founder, governor

74

and all but king of Pennsylvania, we shall single out his uncompromising pacifism, his practical sense and his concern with economy. Like Cruce, he too proposed that young people should be taught "mechanics, a knowledge of nature, to cultivate useful and pleasant arts, and to know the world into which they have been born" rather than how to use arms. He wanted a European passport, and he suggested that the meeting place of the European parliament should be circular, not rectangular, having as many doors as there were delegations, to prevent disputes about precedence . . .

The Abbe de Saint-Pierre

Lastly there is the Plan for Perpetual Peace of the Abbe de Saint-Pierre[11], known chiefly for the derision it aroused throughout the eighteenth century. In six poorly written volumes it contains little that is really new, excepting the proposal that European union should begin with a congress meeting at The Hague— which actually took place 236 years later. This is what Rousseau said about it: "If the plan is not put into execution it will not be because it is fanciful; it is because men are senseless, and because it is a kind of folly to be wise in the midst of fools".[12]

Some of these plans, like Sully's became famous; others, like Saint-Pierre's, were much read: but none of them had the slightest practical result.

The Jacobins

Let us turn the page of the cosmopolitan eighteenth century; Montesquieu, Voltaire and Wieland thought that Europe had already been built, because it existed in their minds and therefore must exist in reality. This brings us to the French Revolution. In 1792 one of its extreme left-wing orators, Anacharsis Cloots, put down at the bar of the Convention a plan for a *Universal Republic*, of which the municipality of Paris would be the all-powerful centre. It was a curious secular replica of Dante's universal monarchy except that, as Cloots made clear, this utopia was to be imposed upon mankind by "war! war! the cry of all patriots scattered over the surface of Europe". The answer to this crusade whose motto would have been "The Jacobins everywhere!" was the completely opposite one of the famous English economist Jeremy Bentham, who incidentally was given French citizenship by the same Convention. His plan was entitled: "A Plan for Perpetual Peace" [13]. His demands included on the one hand that Europe should be neutral, armed and united, on the model of the "Helvetic League", and on the other hand that France and Great Britain should give up their "costly overseas dependencies" as the colonies were then called. Needless to say, the plan was not adopted . . .

Saint-Simon

A little later Count Henri de Saint-Simon, a forerunner of Socialism and of large scale industrial enterprise (the Suez canal was built by his followers) also proposed, in his "Plan for the Organization of European Society" [14] that French and British interests should be merged and that a European parliament elected by leaders in trade and the professions should be set up and "placed over all national governments". Saint-Simon is the real ancestor of the Common Market in that, for him, unity must be born of the "coactive power" of economic institutions, a power which "concerts movements, makes interests common and promises firm".

But once again the age was not realistic enough to understand so clear a message, the message of a political engineer. The industrial age, inaugurated by the libertarian hopes of the democrats, was indeed to see the birth of popular nationalisms, propagated and, above all, induced by the napoleonic conquest. For the Holy Roman Empire and Metternich's Holy Alliance (of kings) it substituted Béranger's ideal of the "Holy Alliance of Peoples". But it was the nation-states which ate the chestnuts pulled out of the fire by such men as Mazzini, Garibaldi, Fourier, Heine, Lamartine and Mickiewicz, all of whom fought for a United States of Europe based upon the will of the peoples—a vision which was hymned by far-sighted poets, and exploited by politicians with short-sighted tricks. The nineteenth century was filled with countless European congresses, and the sum total of their achievement was nothing. But amongst those who attended them was Victor Hugo, that poet who must be acclaimed as the greatest singer of the ideal of European union. He was even acclaimed during his lifetime.

The following is an extract from the report in the *Journal Officiel* of the speech which he made in the French legislative assembly in 1851:

M. HUGO.—The first nation in the world has produced three revolutions, as the gods of Homer took three steps. These three revolutions are one, and it is not a local revolution but the revolution of humanity . . .

After long trials, this revolution gave birth in France to the Republic ... The people of France have carved out of indestructible granite, and placed right in the centre of a continent full of monarchies, the foundation stone of the immense edifice of the future, which will be known one day as the United States of Europe.

M. de MONTALEMBERT.—The United States of Europe! That's going too far. Hugo is mad.

M. MOLE.—The United States of Europe! What an idea! What folly!

M. Quentin-BAUCHARD.—These poets!" [15]

Hugo was not at all put out by these fatheads, whose reactions he had anticipated. He knew the real history of his nation better than many a nationalist. Two years before, at the Peace Congress which met in Paris, he had exclaimed:

"There will come a day when all of you, France, Russia, Italy, Britain, Germany, all you nations of this continent, without losing your distinctive qualities or your glorious individuality, will merge closely into a higher unity and will form the fraternity of Europe, just as Normandy, Brittany, Burgundy, Lorraine, Alsace, all our provinces, have merged to become France. The day will come when the only battlefields will be markets open to commerce and minds open to ideas. The day will come when bullets and bombs will be replaced by votes, by universal suffrage of the peoples and by the true judgement of a great sovereign senate which will be to Europe what Parliament is to England, what the Diet is to Germany and what the Legislative Assembly is to France! The day will come when two huge groups

78

will be seen, the United States of America and the
United States of Europe, holding out their hands to
one another across the ocean, exchanging their products, their trade, their industry, their arts, their
science, reclaiming the globe, colonising deserts and
improving creation under the eye of the Creator
. . ." [16]

Proudhon

In 1868 Proudhon's great prediction appeared: "The
twentieth century will see the beginning of the age of
federations, in which humanity will begin another pur-
gatory lasting a thousand years" [17]. A year previously
Hugo had written: "In the twentieth century, there will
be an extraordinary nation. It will be a great nation, but
at the same time a free one. It will be famous, rich, in-
telligent, peaceful and friendly towards the rest of
humanity. It will have the gravity and charm of an
elder (. . .) The capital of this nation will be Paris, but
the nation will not be called France; its name will be
Europe. It will be called Europe in the twentieth century, but in later centuries, transfigured still further, it
will be called Humanity. Humanity, the ultimate
nation, is even now perceived by thinkers who can pierce
the shadows; but what the nineteenth century is witnessing is the formation of Europe." [18]

Nietzsche versus nationalism

Alas, Hugo was a hundred years ahead of history. For
what the nineteenth century really witnessed was the
triumph of the principle of nationality, as Mazzini said;

and before long this was transformed into militant nationalism, backed by the state and striving for self-sufficiency. Towards the end of the century all percipient observers of these developments—Jacob Burkhardt as much as Dostoievsky, Ernest Renan as much as Nietzsche—were foretelling the worst. Nietzsche wrote in *The Will to Power*: "Let some fresh air in! This absurd state of affairs must not go on any longer in Europe! What sense is there in this bone-headed nationalism? Now that everything points to larger common interests, what is the purpose of encouraging this scurvy egoism?" He believed he could detect "among all the great and deep minds of this century, their common spiritual task consists in preparing for and anticipating this new synthesis: Europe united and the European man of the future."[19] But at the same time he denounced the "paralysis of the will", a sickness threatening to prove fatal to Europe, and from which Russia alone seemed exempt, awaiting her hour . . .

Finally, George Sorel, in one of his *Propos* dated 1912, wrote: "Europe is a cemetery, peopled by nations who sing and then go out to kill one another. Soon the French and the Germans will be singing".[20]

We know what happened. For this was not an empty prophecy!

Just after the first world war, Paul Valéry was able to write: "All is not lost, but everything was touched by the wings of death . . . Now we know that civilization is mortal".[21]

The European Movement 1924

Europe had touched bottom for the first time. It was

then that plans for union began to appear again—there was Count Coudenhove-Kalergi's *Pan Europe*, then Aristide Briand and Alexis Léger, between 1923 and 1932.[22] And as the second world war finished a political, economic and cultural programme was organized with the firm intention of giving immediate effect to expectations which had been denied for more than six centuries.

The time for plans that went unheeded was over. Now things began to happen—many things. Each new step forward had to be cemented by yet another one. Here is the swift chronicle of events:

Resistance in Europe 1944

In the spring of 1944 resistance fighters from nine countries in Europe met four times in secret at a villa in Geneva. They worked out a common declaration giving expression to the united purpose animating those who were in the fight against Nazi oppression. They set out the moral, social, economic and political aims of a union of their countries and they declared:

"These aims can be achieved only if the various countries of the world agree to supersede the dogma of absolute state sovereignty by joining together in a single federal organization. Peace in Europe is the keystone of world peace. For in the space of a single generation Europe has been the epicentre of two world conflicts due primarily to the existence of thirty sovereign states on this continent. This anarchy must be ended by the creation of a federal Union among the peoples of Europe." [23]

You will have recognized in the words of this declaration the main *themes* of the plans I have cited. There is nothing new save for one crucial difference: this time it is not isolated voices separated from one another by twenty or a hundred years, crying in the wilderness and speaking to the future; it is groups of combatants in the thick of the fight; and no longer do they desire: they *will*.

As soon as the war ended, these ideas and wills were translated into action. In all our countries they gave birth to a multitude of movements, groups, associations and leagues committed to the idea of federation. The leaders of these movements met at Montreux in the autumn of 1947[24] and decided to convene a Parliament of Europe for the following spring. Churchill had just made his famous speech at Zurich calling for a union of all the nations of the continent (except the British).[25] He was offered the Presidency of this union.

The Hague Congress 1948

Thus there were brought together a score of federalist or unionist movements, some important statesmen and more than 800 members of parliament, trade union leaders, intellectuals and economists—an unlikely combination, very difficult to bring about, yet accomplished for all that in a few months by an extraordinary moving spirit, the Polish citizen Joseph Retinger.[26] And this conjunction resulted in the *Congress of Europe*, which met at The Hague in May 1948.

It cannot be said too often that everything else flowed from that Congress. For the Hague Congress was the living synthesis of the four traditional themes of union, concretely expressed in its three commissions—political, economic and cultural, representing *peace* through federation, suppressing the anarchy of sovereign states; *prosperity* by means of an economy at once free and organized; and the *spiritual community*, gathering together the living forces of culture, beyond frontiers and nationalisms. What is striking is that the fourth theme, that of *common defence*, which had nearly always figured in the argument up to that time, was quite absent from the discussions and from the final Manifesto.[27]

Everything began at The Hague, I repeat. For, from each of the three themes taken up and crystallized by the congress, in other words from each of the three commissions of which it was made up, there emanated three great series of institutions which to-day are firmly established; three *successes*, in fact: whereas the theme of defence, which was not taken up at The Hague, resulted only in the European Defence Community fiasco of 1954.

(It may be remarked in passing that if, as is often said, fear of Stalin and of communist imperialism was the real reason why we came together, if we federated only under duress, the first institution to be adopted by Europe would logically have been the E.D.C. whereas in fact it was the only one which was rejected.)

Now let us see what was achieved.

The *political commission* at the Hague called for the establishment of a Council of Europe endowed with a Court of human rights and a European Assembly. Nine months later the Council of Europe and the Court were set up. Then the Assembly (unfortunately only consultative) was inaugurated at Strasbourg.

The *economic commission* called for the establishment of common institutions enabling the essential interests of our countries—industrial production, social legislation, customs tariffs, freedom of trade—to be merged. Two years later, Robert Schuman and Jean Monnet put forward their plan for the European Coal and Steel Community (ECSC) which was accepted, and from 1957 Euratom and the Common Market, both of which are forging ahead rapidly, were added.

Lastly, the *cultural commission* called for the setting up of a European Centre of Culture. This was duly created at Geneva in 1949, and during the last dozen years there have grown up around it, often with its help, sometimes without it, at times even in opposition to it (a characteristic result of European pluralism, which is the real foundation of our unity) more than a hundred institutes, associations, European Houses and Foundations[28] all with the object of awakening and sustaining the sense of our common involvement in the spiritual adventure of Europe.

In the economic sphere the movement towards unity seems to be irreversible; already industrialists of their own accord are going far beyond the cautious targets of the treaties. It looks as if this leap forward will soon find official blessing in the political sphere in some form of association, integration or federation. Finally, thanks to the combined efforts of some thirty "University Institutes of European Studies" and of large groups in the educational world, such as the "European Association of Teachers" which operates at primary and secondary school level in some dozen European countries, a feeling for union is taking root among the younger generation. Here indeed is progress! For only so can the building of Europe rest upon broad and firm foundations; only so can the essential transition be effected from the militant will of pioneer groups to the reasoned assent of the majority of citizens. To-day, the leaders are making Europe, tomorrow the people will take over!

In just fifteen years

And all this happened in about fifteen years, during which the vanguard of the united Europe has complained ceaselessly of the indifference with which their appeals were received, and of the scandalous slowness of progress towards Federation! This impatience is necessary. It is one of the essential prerequisites of action of the will to act. Another condition is to know where one is going, which entails establishing where one has come from. In my rapid survey of six and a half centuries of frustration I have tried to recall to you the distant origins and the constant themes of the movement towards union which is now active and gathering momentum before our eyes. In the last section I should like to show you whither this great movement is leading us, can lead us, must lead us. I believe it is leading us to the world, to the final unity of the human race, still following the direction which has always been Europe's true vocation.

1.   D. de Rougemont, *Vingt-Huit Siècles d'Europe* Payot (Bibliothèque Historique), Paris 1961. The quotations from plans for Europe mentioned later on are all taken from this book, where they will be found in their context.

2.   Dante, *De Monarchia*, written in 1308 in Latin. Quotations are from the French translation by B. Landry, Alcan, Paris 1933.

3.   Pierre DuBois, *De recuperatione Terra Sancte*, composed in 1306 and sent as a circular letter to all Christian princes.

4.   Christian L. Lange, *Histoire de l'Internationalisme*, Christiania 1919, vol. I, chapter 4.

5.   The Treaty of George Podiebrad (1420-1471) was written in Latin in the year 1463. The text is reproduced in the *Mémoires* of Philippe de Comines, preceded by this title in French: *Treaty of Alliance and Confederation between King Louis IX, George King of Bohemia and the Seigniory of Venice, to resist the Turk.*

6.   Aeneas Silvius Piccolomini (1405-1464), *De Constantinopolitana clade ac bello contra Turcos congregando.* Podiebrad ascended the throne in 1462, the very year in which Aeneas Silvius became Pope Pius II. These two contemporaries were pursuing the same aim, but Pius II was forced by the antagonism between the Papacy and the Princes to condemn Podiebrad's scheme, which was in fact anti-clerical.

7.   Emeric Crucé (d. 1648): *Le Nouveau Cynée ou discours*

d'Etat representant les occasions et moyens d'établir une paix générale et la liberté du commerce par tout le monde. Published at Paris in 1623.

8. The *Memoires* of Maximilien de Bethune, Duke Sully (their full title takes up a dozen lines) were not published until 1662 although the first two parts were completed in 1638. In 1745 the abbe of Sluys published a short version which was very widely read.

9. Amos Comenius (a latinized form of the name Komenski), 1592-1670 wrote his *Panegersia* or Universal Dream in 1645 and published it in 1666. The sentence quoted is taken from the "Praefatio ad Europeos".

10. The *Essay Towards the Present and Future Peace of Europe* was written between 1692 and 1694, during a break in William Penn's career as a governor.

11. The *Project of Perpetual Peace in Europe* was first published at Cologne in 1712, then at Utrecht in 1713, anonymously. In 1729 the abbé de Saint-Pierre wrote a shorter version, this time over his signature.

12. The *Extrait du Projet de paix perpetuelle de M. l'Abbé de Saint-Pierre, par J.-J Rousseau, citoyen de Genève,* was published at Amsterdam in 1761.

13. It was in his *Principles of International Law,* completed in 1789 and published in 1843, some time after the author's death, that Jeremy Bentham included *A Plan for an Universal and Perpetual Peace,* in which he dealt with the European question.

14. H. de Saint-Simon, *De la réorganisation de la Société européene ou de la necessité de rassembler les peuples de l'Europe en un seul corps politique, en conservant à chacun son indépendence nationale,* Paris 1814.

15. V. Hugo, *Oeuvres complètes,* Actes et Paroles, vol. I, pp. 425-427.

16. V. Hugo, *op. cit.*, I pp. 475-486.

17. P.-J Proudhon, *Oeuvres complètes*, vol. VIII, *Du Principe Federatif*, Paris 1868, p. 177.

18. V. Hugo, *op. cit.*, vol. IV, p. 295. Article entitled: *Il Avenir*.

19. F. Nietzsche, *Beyond Good and Evil*, p. 256, then a posthumous fragment (which we quote) on the same subject.

20. Jean Variot: *Propos de Georges Sorel*, Paris 1935.

21. Paul Valery, *Variete I*, La Crise de L'Esprit (written in 1919) Paris 1924.

22. It was in 1922 that Count Richard Coudenhove-Kalergi first launched in the Austrian and German press a first appeal for the creation of "Paneurope". His *Paneuropean Manifesto* was published in 1924. Aristide Briand, convinced by the young Austrian, decided in 1928 to lay a plan for a European Confederation before the League of Nations. And he entrusted his closest collaborator, Alexis Léger, with the drafting of the *Memorandum on the Organization of a Federal System for Europe*, dated May 1st, 1930 (republished by the *Cahiers de la Pléiade*, special number in honour of Saint-John Perse—Alexis Léger's pseudonym—Paris 1950).

23. See the full text of this declaration by the resistance movements in *L'Europe de Demain*, Editions de la Baconnière, Neuchatel 1945, which gives a detailed account of the secret meetings at Geneva.

24. The documents of the Montreux Congress, 27-31 August 1947, organized by H. Brugmans, Raymond Silva and Alexandre Marc, were published in one volume entitled *Rapport du Premier Congrès annuel de l'Union Européenne des Fédéralistes*, Geneva 1947, now unobtainable.

25. In these words Mr. Churchill made it clear that Britain would not be a member of the Union he was proposing: ". . . France and Germany should together take the lead in this urgent task. Great Britain, the British Empire, powerful America and, I am sure, Soviet Russia—for relations were good at that time—should be friends and guarantors of the new Europe and champions of her right to live." (Cf. *Généalogie des Grands Desseins européens, Bulletin of the* EEC, No. 6, 1960-61, p. 81).

26. On the career of J.-H Retinger, see *Hommage à un grand Européen J.-H. Retinger,* by Prince Bernhard of the Netherlands, Ambassador P. Quaroni, the painter F. Topolski, K. Jelenski, D. de Rougemont, etc., Bulletin of the EEC, No. 5, 1960-61.

27. Text of the Manifesto in *L'Europe en Jeu,* by D. de Rougemont, Ed. de la Baconnière, Neuchatel 1948.

The Congress of Europe was held from the 7th to the 11th May at the Hague under the patronage of Winston Churchill, the Chairman being Duncan Sandys. Chairmen and rapporteurs of the three commissions were: political, Paul Ramadier, Rene Courtin and R. W. G. Mackay; economic, Paul van Zeeland, D. Serruys and Lord Layton; cultural, Salvador de Madariaga and D. de Rougemont.

28. See Raymond Racine, *Les Institutions Culturelles Européenes, inventaire de leurs activites dressé pour la "Fondation européenne de la Culture",* Geneva 1959 (duplicated, 100 copies). This describes sixty governmental and private organizations, university teaching and research (institutions of) or international relations, Foundations, juries for "Prix europeens", etc. Many more institutes have been set up since then.

IV

EUROPE: WHAT OF THE FUTURE?

IV

EUROPE: WHAT OF THE FUTURE?

A new theme: the world

EUROPE, THEN, is in process of uniting and we have
looked at the reasons, both modern and long-standing,
for this. True, there are still three conflicting schools of
thought on the question of political union: that of an
alliance between states, that of total integration, and
that of federation. But there is a new argument which
should force an agreement—the material and moral
need to respond to the appeals which the world makes
to us, on account of its hunger, on account of its fear,
and even on account of its hatred. We must finally
measure up to the demands placed upon us by our
universal vocation.

If it is true that the function creates the organ, this
vocation of *itself* should give us the decisive stimulus
which will compel us to unite the scattered forces of our
nations so as to deploy effectively for the first time in
history, the 'global capacity' of our continent. For it is
the vocation of a man, of a group, or of a culture which
sustains it, enabling it to transcend its native environment and natural endowment—its horoscope. It is its
hope of cheating fate. Having said this, let us take a look
at the prospect that faces us.

This appeal from the world, a consequence of our
own achievements, reaches Europe at a time when, as it
seems to me, her situation is characterized by three

93

determinative factors. Let me describe these factors and how they are related to one another.

The first factor is this: Europe has begun to unite in the very fifteen years in which its individual states have lost their empires.

Decolonization and union

The dates of the successive decolonization of the Near East, India, South-East Asia and Africa are exactly coterminous with the first steps which we took towards union—from 1945 to 1962; and there is every prospect that these two processes will be completed together in a few years from now, the one by the attainment of independence by the few remaining and vestigial colonies and the other by the establishment of common political institutions.

This is a very remarkable coincidence, worthy of serious study. The aim should be to establish whether there are lateral links of cause and effect between the two phenomena or whether, as I believe, they both result from one and the same dialectical evolution, that of nationalism. Ever since the end of the 18th century the disciples of Rousseau, followed by Herder, Bentham and Fichte, had denounced colonial expansion as a mortal sin on the part of Europe, in that it was bound to aggravate the division of the body of Europe into rival nations. And it is certainly true that the necessity alleged by the colonizing states to open up outlets overseas for themselves (*Lebensraum* as Hitler put it) played a considerable part in starting the two world wars. But those wars themselves set in train two series of opposite reactions. On the one hand they gave worldwide

currency to the idea of the right of peoples to self-deter-
mination. The 1914-18 war was fought in the name of
this ideal which was embodied in the 1919 treaties and
was to lead the colonies to claim their own freedom, and
even to discover for themselves the heady effects of
nationalism. On the other hand, however, these same
wars brought home to Europeans that it was high time
that they got their bloodthirsty chauvinism under control; and as we have seen, this led to the rebirth of plans
for union.

Decolonization and prosperity

It is not without interest to underline in passing that
defeatists in Europe, whether nationalist or marxist,
who for fifty years had been saying respectively that
Europe was rich only because she developed her colonies,
or because she plundered them, are being proved wrong
on a scale to which history offers few parallels. For in
fact, if they had been right, the retreat from colonialism
would have signed the death warrant of our economy.
Yet it is plain that this retreat coincides not only with
our union, but also with unprecedented prosperity
throughout the continent. Never before has this Asian
promontory experienced such rapid economic growth
as she has since, willy-nilly, she gave up her overseas
possessions.

Decolonization, union, prosperity—all at once. Here,
briefly, is my explanation of this first fact characterizing
Europe's relations with the world of today.

However criminal one may consider it to have been,
the colonial expansion of rival states did have the effect
of awakening the people of the underprivileged parts of

the World. They came to feel that their traditional mode of life was suffocating them. And they set about demanding the advantages of our civilization, as well as sovereignty for their own states; they did so in the name of some of our finest values—liberty, the worth of the individual and the equality of nations and races—but also in the name of some of our most contagious follies, such as nationalism. And the colonial nations of Europe, twice brought to the verge of ruin by the mania of nationalism, were compelled to weigh things up again. Yielding to the pressure of a world opinion which their own principles had created, and of a new class which they had educated in the countries they colonized, yielding also to their own enlightened self-interest— and with a little urging from the United States, which at the time was saving them from bankruptcy, one after another they "disengaged". But at the same time, and for the same reasons, they admitted what they had refused to admit for nearly six and a half centuries— that they must unite. They lost the world and found Europe again.

Europe withdraws to her advantage

But the second dominant feature of our situation is just as paradoxical. It is this: *Europe's political retreat coincides with the accelerated adoption of our civilization by the under-privileged nations.*

As I said at the beginning, Europe has made the world, not only by discovering the whole of its surface but supremely by giving the world its first really universal civilization.

"*Colonialism*"

We all know that this civilization is held responsible, rightly or wrongly, for as many evils as benefits. Nonetheless it is the only one which has succeeded in becoming exportable and assimilable beyond the context of its racial, political and religious origins. The means by which it was carried all over the world since the Reformation are matters of history, and they were not all Christian! Animated by the most diverse motives—missionary, commercial, political or simply by love of adventure, without any order or concerted plan, from the sixteenth to the nineteenth centuries Europeans established churches and offices, cities and industries, schools and plantations, newspapers and parliaments on every continent. Conquering by force or received as Gods—like Cortez in Mexico—anxious to save souls or exploit mines, they conquered, civilized, pillaged, evangelized, engaged in the slave trade, opened hospitals, disseminated humanitarian theories which they themselves did not always fully practise, imprisoned those who dare to quote their principles against them, but at the same time freed whole peoples inured for centuries to living under the most cruel indigenous oppression. Nowadays all this is lumped together in one word: colonialism. I know of nothing more unfair, since it is given an exclusively pejorative connotation, whereas it covers an immense process which included humanity and heroic love just as much as crime and greed. It is an adventure which has not yet been put into true perspective, and there is nothing to prove that in the end the benefits will not outweigh the evils. For it is a story of progress as conceived in the West; a progress adopted even by those who denounce the West.

Never before has there been a world civilization like ours. The historian Toynbee will contradict me here, saying that Alexander the Great and the Chinese emperors also ruled what they believed to be the entire world. Well, they were mistaken, that's all! Even Cook's travel agency could put them right on that score nowadays. The World is now known in all its physical dimensions, and such monumental errors are no longer possible. The main features of its history have also been explored, and Western archaeology is tirelessly disinterring more traditions *forgotten by their own peoples* than our armies and our missions have ever destroyed or changed.

But will not the "Europeanization" of the world gradually fade away as a result of the European withdrawal known as "decolonization?" It is hard to judge, since the retreat has not yet been concluded. But all verifiable signs point towards a pronounced tendency for our culture to extend its influence in the liberated colonies.

India without the British

The withdrawal of the British from India was not followed by the rejection of parliamentary government on the British model. Instead it was adopted immediately root and branch. On the other hand, the caste system which had lasted for three thousand years, and which the British had left intact, was abolished. Political parties proliferated, heavy industry was developed and birth control began to be adopted. . . . Altogether, independent India wants to be more British, which means more Western, than ever she was as a part of the Empire. She may be wrong, but that is the situation.

Africa after the French

European culture and languages are making spectacular progress in the recently liberated countries of Black Africa. In January 1961 the French director of cultural affairs said: "In Cambodia all the young people speak French, whereas when men now forty or fifty were growing up, under colonialism, only the leaders knew our language. . . . People no longer learn French in these countries because they are compelled to do so, but because they need the language, because it has become a factor of national cohesion, and furthermore because it facilitates entry into international life. . . ." Here, as elsewhere, interest seems to be a more effective spur than constraint.

And everywhere among the emergent nations, as soon as our armies and administrators have left, laws have been passed for the immediate adoption of political, social, health, town-planning, technical and industrial measures which were quite simply copies of Western laws on these matters. What is more, the only reason why the administrators left was that the leaders among the native populations had adopted European ideals. These ideals are now used against us, and against our practices which too often have been immoral; they must be worth more than we knew, worth more than we are: so much the worse for us—but so much the better for our ideals! For my part, I see no threat to them in de-colonization—quite the contrary. Never before have

Europe and the West made such progress in the souls and the culture of peoples who but yesterday were still under colonialism.

Lack of wise control

But the third dominant feature is this: *our ideals and practices were disseminated in an unregulated way, without any plan or wise overall direction.*

Two sets of consequences have resulted from this fact, and they may ultimately be as unfortunate for us Europeans as for the emergent nations.

First unfortunate for us. For it is plain that our civilization has made itself transportable and assimilable only at the cost of a dangerous dissociation between its *products* of every kind and its fundamental *values*. The world accepts our machines and some of our slogans, but not the religious, philosophical and cultural background which besides producing science and technology also enabled us to integrate them, over a period, into the complex of our customs and our human equilibria. It has to be admitted that simplified versions of Western civilization lend themselves more easily to export than does the original version. This is what gives the Americans and even more the Russians, their great advantage when it is a question of modernizing—that is to say Westernizing—rapidly and on a large scale the newly liberated colonies. These newcomers bring much simpler ideas of progress, to the emergent nations, whether on the purely material plane or on the social and moral level. The former do not have the scruples and the uneasy conscience which marked European ruling circles during the last days of the colonial era, whilst the latter have never been inhibited by any regard for in-digenous cultures, either within their own empire or in Africa or Asia.[1] In the short run, therefore, their chances may appear more favourable than ours, for the emer-gent nations are not predisposed against them. They do not say of their gifts, as they do of ours: "this is neo-colonialism". And yet the emergent nations have far more to lose in this matter than we have—as the best minds among them are finding out. But when they do, they heap reproaches upon us.

Europe the accused

In this connection I shall quote to you an Indian professor teaching at Oxford, Dr. Raghavan Iyer. Quite recently, speaking at a congress in Europe, he set out to interpret the resentment felt by the emergent countries with regard to our culture and the disorderly way in which it was propagated. He pointed out that the under-developed countries imitate clumsily everything that the West has done, and blamed Europe for all the evils resulting from this, as well as for the reappearance in Asia and Africa of what he called "unbalanced or out-moded conceptions of the mind of Europe". He gave the following impressive list of these evils: "The gospel of inevitable material progress, an aggressive nationalism, that reached the level of scarcely veiled racial hatred, Benthamite utilitarianism, militant collectivism and messianic Socialism, liberalism of the Hayek variety, the worship of military and political power, a bureaucracy by now ineradicable, the multiplication of new wants, consumption on a colossal scale, a passion for strange things, claims to exclusivity in religion, ideological fanaticism, arrogant atheism, the cult of cynicism, un-bridled and cultural philistinism."[2]

This is quite an impressive list of our vices, or at least of their manifestations since the beginning of the indus-trial era. It would be too facile a rejoinder to those who speak thus to say "Why didn't you adopt our virtues, which could be just as easily listed? And, in general, why do you imitate us? Why do you reproach us with our atheism and still more with our materialism, when you are loudly demanding material aid, not missionaries from us?"

The guilt of Europe

This would be too facile a reply, since we are largely responsible for the mistakes which the underprivileged nations make when they pass judgement on us. We do not send overseas the best representatives of our civiliza-tion, those who are most conscious of Europe's true values; we send representatives of our governments and our firms, who take with them all our rivalries; we send out workers in technical aid programmes who know little of the country in which they are going to work, and still less about the overall impression which Europe may make when seen from a distance; we send out political agitators, uncultured businessmen and our worst films. We send out a shower of our by-products, our adventurers and our books, our national quarrels, our machinery and our dogmas, with the most utter and complete irresponsibility, heedless alike of their culture and our own.

Need for a policy of civilization

That is Europe's real situation in to-day's world. To sum up: decolonization, far from ruining us, has coincided with our union, which gives promise of an unprecedented prosperity. The whole world is learning from our civilization; but it is not by any means taking from us the best we have to give, and its attitude towards us is compounded of condemnation and jealousy. Ultimately this is our fault, since we have never worked out a *policy of civilization* adequate to meet the demands of the century and our worldwide responsibilities.

This being so, the question we have to answer is whether Europe's values are to be supplanted by her most saleable products and her most demagogic slogans, to the sole advantage of those who most skilfully manage and exploit them. Is she going to be pushed out by the underprivileged nations because of her vices, at the expense of her authentic virtues? Or has she still the material and moral resources wherewith to act once more?

Defeatism in Europe

There is a certain streak of defeatism in Europe, running from Spengler to Toynbee, and from Sorel to Sartre[3], which appears to have persuaded both the masses and their leaders in our countries that Europe is a poor creature crushed between two colossi. This belief, or fear, has haunted our minds since the eighteenth century yet it seems to be curiously at variance with the facts. On the eve of the French Revolution, Baron Grimm, a literary journalist in Paris, wrote to Catherine of Russia: "Two empires will divide the world between them: Russia in the East and America, which has gained its freedom in recent years, in the West; and we, the people in between, shall be too degraded, we shall have sunk too low, to know, except through vague and incoherent tradition, what we have been." [4]

In 1847, Sainte-Beuve summarized the opinion of the historian Adolphe Thiers as follows: "There are only two nations left. Russia, still barbarous, but great . . . old Europe will have to reckon with this *youth*. The other young country is America . . . the future of the world is there, between those two great worlds." [5] And a score of others throughout the nineteenth century, and thus well before the achievement of great power status by these two nations (which dates exactly from the end of the second world war), said the same thing. Europe felt herself to be crushed between the two great colossi which had yet to arise. Well, now they are here; so let us take their real measure.

"Europe between the two Great Powers"
A platitude:

I have invented a little drawing game. It's very easy. Take a sheet of graph paper. Draw on it three vertical rectangles placed side by side, each one being ten squares wide. The one on the left is eighteen squares high, and the right-hand one is twenty-two squares. The centre one is forty-three squares high; therefore it is larger than both the others added together. Question: What does this centre square mean? Answer: It is Europe between the two Great Powers. Each square represents a million inhabitants. Europe west of the

Iron Curtain has 330 million; the seven European states now subject to Soviet Russia have 95 millions, making a total of 425 millions, whilst the two Great Powers together have scarcely 400 millions.[6]

Add to this demographic quantity the human qualities of the European, who is still the best worker, the best philosopher and the best artist, and you will admit that it is at least curious that Europe should feel herself to be crushed between two colossi smaller than herself, who would not reach her height even if they stood one on top of the other and who, into the bargain, far from joining forces against us are rivals, one of them being our ally.

Do I hear you telling me that the real power of Europe is not proportional to her population? That is correct, in the sense that production per head of the population in America is greater than that in Europe. But the rate of growth in Europe is much greater than that in America. And if we come to absolute figures, Europe occupies first place as a producer of steel, cast iron, coal, cement, butter and milk, which are primary products, the United States holding second place and Russia third. So much for quantity. It is clearly a more difficult matter to evaluate quality precisely. But here is a statistic which to my mind is not without significance: production of first class scholars, calculated in Nobel Prizes for the sciences, from 1901, when the prize was first offered, to 1961: Russia and people's democracies, 9 prizewinners; United States, 52; Western Europe 147; other countries, 8.[7]

But, you will still reply, those figures are abstractions! I *still* feel crushed . . .[9] Quite right! You don't yet feel as if you belonged to a nation of 335 millions, or even

430 millions, counting the countries which are still satellites of the USSR; you just feel like a citizen of a little country of 5, 10 or 50 millions, which is not on the right scale for the modern world. Yes, United Europe has not yet been created, and it is imperative to create her so that our global capacity may come to life not only in statistics but also in our consciousness.

Europe has everything she needs to become once again the premier power in the world, not on account of her dimensions but on account of her demographic, economic and cultural potential.

Nevertheless, the fate of a civilization does not depend only on considerations of that kind. It depends quite as much on its active vocation, by which I mean the conscious acceptance of this vocation by those who are responsible for so doing; it also depends upon the strength of other cultures or civilizations which are competing for the succession.

You are well aware that many intellectual leaders in the West despair very vocally of our values and deny that the West, as represented by Europe which is in the process of uniting, and by the United States, has any vocation at all. One often hears it said that the West is in the throes of moral decline, and specifically that it no longer has an ideal with which to combat the new, all-conquering values of communism.

My answer to that is to refer you to the facts once more. The West's economic prosperity and intellectual vitality, nowhere surpassed or even remotely approached either in the East or in Africa, are indicative of renaissance, not of decadence. But there is more. We are told that the new values, able to attract the world and give it a new ideal, are those represented by communist

Russia. I look—but I see nothing new. For what, after all, *is* Soviet communism? A mixture fifty per cent of which stems from traditions which are peculiarly Russian and even Tzarist, such as the role of the police and of the bureaucrats, internal passports, an ubiquitous censorship or the habit cf rewriting history every time the policy of the ruler or Party in power has to be justified;[8] and the other fifty per cent is more or less faithfully applied marxism. But marxism was not invented in Russia. Popov didn't create it—Karl Marx did. And who was Marx? A German Jew whose father had become a Protestant, and who wrote articles for the *New York Herald Tribune* whilst living in England. (These articles, when collected later on, formed several chapters of *Das Kapital*[9].) Marx is one of the most typical products of the philosophical, theological and political disputes of the nineteenth century. So the Russians are in fact returning to us our own values in the guise of dialectical marxism—very much simplified and impoverished, at that.

Where are the successors?

Should we then look for another hypothetical successor to take from our feeble hands what used to be called "the torch of civilization?" There again, I don't see one. I cannot see a single culture independent of our own, fundamentally different from ours, and potentially more capable than we of exercising the function of worldwide unification which henceforth, in the technical age, will be the first charge laid upon a civilization. On the contrary, one look around the world shows us that the newly emergent nations are turning towards

Europe, even though they may hurl insults as they imitate her. Here is a brief summary of my observations: South East Asia is jealous of China and would secretly like to imitate her; but China is trying to catch up with Russia, hoping to beat her on her own ground; Russia for her part has been saying for the last thirty years that she will do better than America—but America, after all, was made by Europe! The circle closes, and we are brought back to Europe.

Europe responsible—
in the active sense

Where, in all this, is our successor to be found? I can see only imitators, some way behind us, who very often caricature our worst faults. No, we cannot escape from our vocation on the pretext of our weakness, or of those crimes of a recent past for which the underprivileged nations hold us responsible. For, as I have shown, this weakness is due entirely to the fact that our forces are divided, not to any lack of potential power; and we are now in the process of joining forces again. And those crimes, which were those of our nationalisms, of racialism, and to a certain extent of colonialism, demand of us something very different from an impatient masochistic *mea culpa*, which is so much easier than action. Europe's virtues and vices, her past and her experience, make her doubly *responsible*—in the active meaning of the word, this time—for facing the world and accepting a vocation in which nobody can replace her and which, in my view, no other culture and no other system has the resources to discharge if Europe refuses it.

Europe's worldwide vocation

This vocation, as I like to call it, or this worldwide function if you prefer, can I think be summed up in these three verbs: *animate, balance, federate.*

In saying a few words about them I shall be summarising at the same time the substance of this book.

1. *To animate or quicken*

First of all, to animate or quicken international exchanges. This is self-evident as regards the exchange of material goods, since Europe created and established world trade immediately after the Great Discoveries and only with the techniques which she invented can it be maintained. Europe is still the heart of any system of worldwide exchange, not only because of the place she holds at the centre of the privileged world (about which I wrote in Chapter 2), but because the value of her international trade is more than twice that of the United States and nearly ten times that of the USSR. Europe's worldwide vocation is confirmed by facts such as the following: exports account for some forty per cent of our trade and imports represent a similar figure, whilst the United States depends on the rest of the world to the extent of not more than five per cent of its national product. The world is vital to Europe; it is less so to the United States, and much less still to Russia as she now is.

As regards cultural, not to speak of spiritual, exchange, I may perhaps be allowed to speak from practical experience. Everything marks out Europe as the place where these may be initiated and directed towards a fruitful dialogue. First there are our traditions, not only of curiosity but also of respect for spiritual values, even (sometimes supremely) when they are different from our own; it was not by accident that Europe created ethnology and archaeology and the science of comparative religions of which, before her time, no trace was found on the earth. In all these things America is giving very powerful help, but the initiative came from Europe and it is towards her that I can see the leaders of the underprivileged nations turning with naturalness. It is through Europe that they become aware of the need and the means to engage in dialogue, not only with us, but also with one another.

2. *Balance*

The second aspect of Europe's vocation is that of establishing a balance among the things which mankind has created—between technology and tradition, for example.

It was in Germany, Britain, France and Switzerland that industrial techniques originated at the beginning of the nineteenth century, and it was in these countries that they encountered resistance from tradition and custom which compelled them slowly to adapt themselves to the rhythms of life. Overall the pace of adaptation was very slow but there were some significant offshoots which included socialism, marxism, liberalism, Trades Unionism, planning, and vocational guidance and training . . . This adaptation, though painful, was also fruitful. At the beginning there were workers' revolts in Lyons or Zurich against power looms, later against mass production in America, and quite recently against automation in Coventry. All this represents a fund of human experience from which the emergent countries should be able to learn a great deal. For these countries insist on having our beautiful machinery, not suspecting that little by little it can destroy their most treasured traditions and their psychic equilibria through the invisible fields of force accompanying it, just as the wooden horse of Troy did.

Then there are so many other equilibria between extremes which I have had occasion to mention when dealing with many varied aspects of life in Europe; the balance between authority and liberty, between science and the humanities, in education; between critical aggressiveness and poetical imagination in the sciences; between pure tones or separate voices and combined harmonies in the arts; between innovation and continuity in civic life, and between diversity and unity in political organization; and first, but also last, between the passion for adventure heedless of the consequences, and for experience stored up and meditated upon which together made up the wisdom of Ulysses, the proto-European.

3. *Federate*

This brings us naturally to the third verb which typifies our vocation, namely to *federate*.

To vindicate federalism by example is perhaps the greatest task for which the West carries the responsibility, both to the underprivileged world and to herself. For it was Europe which spread the virus of nationalism all round the world—this disease which has twice proved nearly fatal to herself. And this feverish sickness now plagues nearly all the underprivileged nations, inciting them to the worst excesses of chauvinism and to political and economic actions which are clearly against their own interests, but which they insist on taking *for the sake of prestige*.[10] On the pretext of freeing themselves from the last traces of our imperialism, all too often they copy its most glaring faults. So Europe is in honour bound to produce, to prove and then to disseminate the antibody of this fatal virus which we have inherited from the nineteenth century.

But the antidote to nationalism and chauvinism whether based on race or class, and ultimately to the totalitarian dictatorships which are its inevitable product in this century, is to hold federalist beliefs and put them into practice. It is to establish unity in diversity, an organic balance between local freedoms and communal obligations, and the pooling of "sovereign" rights which none of our countries is able to exercise alone in the present-day world.

A pattern for the world

So Europe's vocation whose fulfilment she owes to-day to the world of to-morrow is to show it a Federation working successfully on a grand scale. It may be that the connection which I noted earlier between the ending of our colonial imperialism, the beginnings of federal union in Europe, and the expansion of our economy, holds an important lesson not only for the underprivileged nations but also, and perhaps primarily, for the West as a whole, including America and Russia—a West that *must* overcome its differences. This could come about even in the present generation if Europe,

whence the disease spread, succeeded in uniting in freedom, thus completing her adventure and making the
world in making herself. *This* is the new ideal for which
our youth is looking—a federated Europe, a pattern
for the world.

The time has passed when we could doubt our western
values and not be ashamed of so doing. No, the time
has come to take them seriously ourselves. We simply
have no right to meet the expectancy of the younger
nations and of the youth of Russia, who are looking to
the West more than we think, with a sickly and mealy-
mouthed *mea culpa*. To them we represent a hope which
we dare not disappoint.

And so I end.

The future of Europe will be founded upon great geo-
economic realities that now have worldwide ramifica-
tions. I believe too that it will be based on a universal
purpose whose roots descend to our cultural past, and
are embedded in the basic facts about the West, a
purpose demanded by the logic of world events in this
second half of the twentieth century.

It is this vocation which will be our main source of
strength if we assume it *now*, and resolutely put into
practice a *worldwide policy of civilization*. The prospects
for Europe do not depend upon a correct guess as to
what others will do. They depend upon the spirit that
activates our deeds. No longer may we seek anxiously
to *guess* what history holds next in store for us; our
calling is to *make* history.

1. In 1916 Lenin said, in "Imperialism, the last stage of Capitalism", that Russia was the second largest colonial power in the world judging by the extent of her empire, and he enumerated her possessions: Azerbaijan, Armenia, Georgia, Uzbekistan, Kazakhstan, Turkmenistan, Tsdjikistan, Kirghizia, eight countries in which a majority of the population was Mohammedan. Since then the USSR has added three colonies—the Baltic states—to her empire, and Stalin tightened the screws considerably on the "sister republics". During this same period Europe was "decolonizing", not because of communism (which played some part in the process only in Viet Minh) but in the name of her own guiding principles. And so the Russia of Lenin's heirs has now no rival as the *first* colonial power in the world. Before long she will be, though in a different sense, the only one and the last.

2. See the documents of the conference held by the *Fondation Européene de la Culture* in April 1962 at Brussels, in "Caractere et Culture de l'Europe", No. 7.

3. Cf. *The Decline of the West* by Oswald Spengler, and *The World and the West* by Arnold Toynbee. Georges Sorel said in 1908: "Europe is the seat of warlike upheavals par excellence. . . . There is no hope for her . . . Unhappy Europe! why hide her coming fate from her? Within ten years she will go down in war and anarchy."

And in 1912: "Nothing will alleviate Europe's lot. . . .
Europe, this cemetery. . . ." Fifty years later, J.-P
Sartre writes: "Europe is done for. . . . She is very likely
to collapse . . . she is leaking everywhere . . . this is the
end". (See appendix: "Sartre against Europe").

4. Letter written by Melchior Grimm to Catherine II
in 1790, the year in which Grimm left Paris to enter
Russia's service.

5. Sainte-Beuve, *Cahiers*, note of 1847. Similar pro-
phecies by Jean de Muller in 1797, by Napoleon
(Memorial de Saint-Helene), by the abbe de Pradt in
1823 ("Beyond the Vistula a curtain is falling"), by
Henry Adams in 1900, and above all by de Tocqueville
in 1856, are quoted in my *Vingt-Huit Siècles d'Europe*.
("There are two great nations in the world to-day . . .
each of them seems destined to hold in its hands one
day the fate of half the world."), cf. pp. 268 to 276 of
op. cit.

6. The population figures for Western Europe differ
by several millions according to the sources. A work as
conscientiously researched as *Europe's Needs and Resources*,
published in November 1961 by the Twentieth Century
Fund, of New York, gives the following data:

    1952: 289.16 million; 1955: 295.17; 1958: 302.16

Since the rate of increase is accelerating, this would give
a total of more than 313 million in 1962; and the above
projections have already proved too conservative. To
them I add Yugoslavia with 17 million, making 330
million. If one goes by the results of the latest censuses,
e.g. that of France in 1961, these figures would appear to
fall short by some millions.

    Present estimates place the total population of Eastern
Europe (the seven USSR satellites) at 95 million.

Latest population figures for the USA and the USSR are 179.5 and 220 millions respectively.

7. cf. "La nationalité des Prix Nobel de Science de 1901 a 1960, essai d' analyse sociologique", by Leo Moulin, Cahiers Internationaux de la Sociologie, Presses Universitaires Francaises 1961.

8. See on this point the well-known memoirs of the Marquis de Custine, published at Paris in 1843: *La Russie en* 1839, which has many detailed examples of tzarist police measures identical with those which were used under Stalin; of bureaucracy run mad, falsification of history, and of dictatorship of the mind in general. "Here, even the mind is regimented. . . . Here to lie is to protect the State, and to tell the truth is subversion . . . the Government dominates everything and inspires nothing . . . everybody thinks what nobody dares say", etc.

9. The 500-odd articles which Marx, with the help of Engels, sent to the New York *Herald*, which later became the *New York Herald Tribune*, between 1851 and 1861, were republished in part in 1897 under the title: *The Eastern Question*. Several critical studies of them have recently been published in the United States.

10. *Le Dialogue des Cultures*, recently published by Editions de la Baconnière for the EEC, gives many good examples of these processes both in the economic and political sphere, which are mentioned particularly by Prof. Ebrahim Madkour and B. de Jouvenel.

APPENDIX

Sartre versus Europe

APPENDIX

Sartre versus Europe

I HAVE just spent two months in the United States, and everybody is talking about the miracle of Europe. Daily newspapers, weeklies, reviews, weighty books, universities and government circles in Washington are becoming aware of United Europe. To listen to them, one would think the task was completed. Great Britain's application to join the Common Market suddenly alerted them. The Common Market—that was Jean Monnet's creation, they thought, which was simplifying things a little; and the Common Market must be working because Great Britain, which once treated it with disdain, later asked to be allowed to join. So Jean Monnet was the true prophet. Therefore we must see Europe as he first envisaged it—as the first step towards an organization of the world in which Europe would be both the centre of inspiration and the element of balance.

I came back to Europe—"our homeland", as Aeneas Silvius said in the fifteenth century—and glanced through what was being written on this subject. Dozens and dozens of works had been published during those two months, in all our languages, about the integration of Europe and the new relationships which had to be established between a united Europe and the under-privileged world. They were full of ideas and figures, and instinct with sober optimism and constructive realism. The rate of growth of production and exports was beating all records. Despite increasing automation, unemployment had disappeared except in Italy. In the new atmosphere of confidence born of the promise of the Common Market and of its first successes, industrial agreements were proliferating within and across national frontiers. The OECD forecast that in ten years' time an overall expansion of 50 per cent would have occurred in the economies of the Atlantic Group. So America must be right!

But I found one publication—just one—which rudely contradicted all the rest. It said that Europe was "done for", that she was "in grave danger of collapse", that she was "in her dying convulsions", that she was "leaking everywhere", that she was "at rock bottom", that "this is the end", and that here we are all "in chains, humiliated and sick with fear". Now those were not the words of an expert wedded to facts, but of an eloquent moralist, Jean-Paul Sartre; and his fierce anger is due not to his having studied the evidence, but to his having read a pamphlet. In a preface which he has written to it, he exhorts "Europeans" to read it, and his reasoning is as follows: all Europeans are accomplices of colonialism which is criminal; therefore, on reading this pamphlet they will be ashamed, and shame is an incentive to revolution. Revolution, he continues, cures all ills by the *violence* which seizes its instigators, and which its victims are able to liberate. So let us make common cause with the FLN, the Angolans and other Balugas who "kill Europeans at sight". For by so doing they are "makers of human history", and so we shall be on the right side.

I am not making this up—only quoting and condensing this humanitarian dialectic which offers us a "means of curing Europe" by making us all go over to the enemy camp. All they have to do "in order to become men" is to kill us; it's in black and white, on page 17. The worst that can happen is that there will be nobody left to shoot; and then, of course, there will be no more wars. The rude logic of this new plan for perpetual peace is bound to fascinate some specimens of youth who are "sick of our values" and are loudly demanding that we be brainwashed.

"For centuries, Europe has crushed nearly the whole of humanity in the name of a so-called spiritual adventure". This sentence sums up the argument of the writer of the publication, Frantz Fanon of Martinique. Sartre quotes it and then adds, much impressed: "This is a new note."

What impresses me is not the note, which is hardly newer than communist propaganda this forty years past, but the content of the sentence: there is not a word of truth in it.

Colonization by the whites has not lasted "for centuries" in Africa, but, on the average, approximately eighty years—from 1882 to the present as far as nine-tenths of the continent is concerned.

This colonization was not undertaken "in the name of a so-called spiritual adventure" (by no means "so-called", either) but for other, more material reasons, not all of which are to our shame. The first and most important of these was an *actual situation* not of Europe's making and which, far from being the result of colonialism, as M. Fanon says again, made it possible, even inevitable; I mean the condition of economic, social and political backwardness of those regions which became colonies for a while, and which are now rapidly advancing before our very eyes, after centuries of immobility and constant decadence.

What did Europe "crush" in the underprivileged regions she colonized? (And they are far from being "almost the whole of humanity", but at the most one-third of it, during the period under consideration). Did she crush the culture of India? She saved it. African industry? She established it. Democracy in Saudi Arabia or the Yemen? Respect for the person among cannibals? You want to laugh, but you can't.

It is very wrong of M. Fanon, seconded by J.-P. Sartre, to shout about "centuries of oppression". Before letting them make History, one might advise them to learn it.

Here is the history of a nation recently freed from European "oppression"—Dahomey.

The first contacts which Dahomey had with European civilization go back to 1729, when King Agaja and his regiment of women, having beaten the Popos with the aid of the Englishman Testefole, captured the seaport of Ouidah. They massacred everyone there and set up a new office in the state, known as "Yevogan" ("he who deals with the whites"). This was translated "with all the appropriate diplomatic emphasis, as Minister of Foreign Affairs". All this is to be found in the *Histoire des peuples d'Afrique noire*, published by Robert Cornevin. Agaja's successors enriched themselves through the slave trade; they drew their supplies from a neighbouring tribe, paid tribute to the Yorubas, recouped themselves by taxing the Houedas and by fighting the Popos from time to time. In 1884, Gregoire's dictionary described the country as follows: "The soil is extremely fertile and is covered with forests. Unhappily industry and agriculture are stifled by the frightful despotism to which the country is subject. The king, who receives a kind of worship, is noted for horrible human sacrifices. He has an army of women. Dahomey has less than a million inhabitants, and scarcely 20,000 are free. There is a French settlement on the coast."

This happy country was first colonized in 1892, a condition which ended in 1960 with the creation of a sovereign republic of more than 2 million people, whose president was received with great ceremony at the Elysée palace in 1961.

I leave Messrs. Sartre and Fanon to prove that this example does not invalidate their case at all, or doesn't count. I leave them to prove by dialectics that the kingdom of Ghana and the empire of Mali were not destroyed by the almoravid Arabs and then by the Moroccan sultans, but by the Europeans, who simply occupied, several centuries later and for just sixty-six years, these remnants of states previously invaded and subjugated by the Touaregs and the Peuls. I also leave them to prove (it will be some job, this) that India was freed from the British by violence alone, in accordance with their favourite theory; for otherwise, it isn't worth much. This won't worry them, for passion does not worry about facts, and their passion demands death for the guilty, who is of course the European and no-one else.

But if we keep to the facts and make use of historical perspective, the truth is that notwithstanding its crimes, colonialism has awakened the peoples of the under-privileged world in the very short space of three generations. It has made them see such possibilities of development that they realized they were suffocating under their traditional modes of life. Fired by some of our values, such as equality, liberty, the dignity of the person and the right to education, as well as by some of our most contagious follies, nationalism and ideological hatred, those peoples have set about claiming the advantages of our civilization, and sovereignty for their states as well. As for the colonialist countries of Europe—seven out of twenty-six at the end of the war —twice nearly ruined by their mad disease of nationalism and compelled to take stock afresh, they yielded to the threefold pressure of a world public opinion formed by their principles, of a new class which they had educated in the colonized countries, and of enlightened self-interest—to which was added some pressure from the United States, which was saving them from bankruptcy at the time: and, one after another they pulled out.

What has become of Europe considered as a whole? *Europe was literally created by the underprivileged nations*, writes Fanon. She grew rich by stealing, i.e. by exploiting the soil of Africa and Asia—gold, metals, petrol, rubber. (Is the countryman created by his land and the riches it contains?) Sartre goes further, and says that these riches built not only Europe's industrial capital, but her cathedrals! (Yes, it's there on page 23.) Moreover, "Europeans became men only by making slaves" (what! weren't they human before the sixteenth century?). So by leaving the oppressed countries, Europe must have signed her economic death-warrant and set her feet on the road to swift dehumanization? Were the opponents of colonialism advocating suicide for Europe? Then what were the values, dearer than life itself, that inspired them? Their own "rotten" European values? If not, which others? But let us leave these digressions and come back to the facts.

The fact is that no sooner had the countries of Europe been freed from the crippling burden of their colonies than they became aware of *Europe* herself, and their need to unite. What is more, the beginnings of Europe's unity —for the Common Market is not yet five years old— have witnessed an almost immediate and stupendous upsurge of prosperity. Europe is not "finished," with all due deference to our wild men. She has hardly begun, and her growth is phenomenal.

So much the worse for Fanon and his marxism—he borrowed it from Europe anyway. But why is Sartre mixed up in this sad affair? This anachronism calls for an explanation.

Sartre is intellectually a provincial who projects his petty grievances against "Europe". When he writes Europe he is thinking only about France, and when he thinks of France he sees nothing but the Algerian tragedy. "Let us leave our province—I mean our nation", one would like to keep repeating to him; and it is not my fault that this sentence was used by Michel Debré in his *Projet de pacte pour une union des Etats d'Europe* published by Nagel in 1950.

Sartre's diatribe comes a little too late, for nobody now defends the system he is attacking—not even the Russians, who still practise it. In fact, his preface is no more than an appendix—a needless one at that—to the long tradition of the best minds who found it possible to condemn colonialism in its earliest days, and who did so not in opposition to Europe but *in the name of European values*: Voltaire, Rousseau, Herder, Fichte, Bentham. Unlike Hegel, who considered Europe "the real end of

History", and Auguste Comte who saw in her "the privilege rightly due to the most outstanding development of society", these philosophers believed themselves to be serving our true values by putting us on guard against our inevitable expansion—unsuccessfully, as it happened. All they did was to safeguard our principles, compromised or betrayed by our practice. But now the colonial period has ended, for reasons they could not foresee. So why continue to rail, except for the pleasure of wallowing in one's own masochism, or simply to annoy de Gaulle? And even he presided, not without dignity, over the dissolution of a colonial empire.

We have better things to do than to utter wails of self-condemnation to satisfy our personal complexes.

Faced with the economic crisis and the nationalistic fever of the underprivileged nations, and with deep movements of thought in the USSR, we may no longer spit upon our values. We have to take them seriously ourselves, and draw from them the practical conclusions both for the under-privileged nations and for Europe whose task is to help them. When youth under the Soviets and elsewhere looks half-consciously towards us, it must not look in vain.

What we must offer to the world and to the younger generation is not our bad conscience, our flagellant urges or the collective renunciation of our past, but proof that we have succeeded in outgrowing nationalism, and therefore colonialism, by uniting in a grand federation.

Those who will lose face in the eyes of future generations are those who were saying that Europe was finished, when they should have been helping to build her.